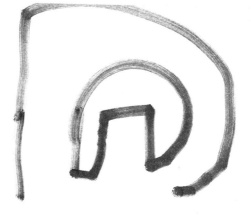

PRAYING THE HOURS
in ordinary life

PRAYING THE HOURS
in ordinary life

LAURALEE FARRER *and* CLAYTON J. SCHMIT
ILLUSTRATIONS BY DENISE LOUISE KLITSIE
TRANSLATIONS BY MARTINA NAGEL

CASCADE BOOKS
AN IMPRINT OF WIPF AND STOCK PUBLISHERS, EUGENE, OR

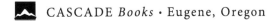 CASCADE *Books* · Eugene, Oregon

Art for Faith's Sake series

SERIES EDITORS: Clayton J. Schmit
                    J. Frederick Davison

This series of publications is designed to promote the creation of resources for the church at worship. It promotes the creation of two types of material, what we are calling primary and secondary liturgical art.

   Like primary liturgical theology, classically understood as the actual prayer and practice of people at worship, primary liturgical art is that which is produced to give voice to God's people in public prayer or private devotion. Secondary liturgical art, like secondary theology, is written reflection on material that is created for the sake of the prayer, praise, and meditation of God's people.

   The series presents both worship art and theological and pedagogical reflection on the arts of worship. The series title Art for Faith's Sake* indicates that, while some art may be created for its own sake, a higher purpose exists for arts that are created for use in prayer and praise.

*Art for Faith's Sake is a phrase coined by art collector and church musician Jerry Evenrud, to whom we are indebted.

Cataloging-in-Publication data:
Farrer, Lauralee
Praying the Hours in Ordinary Life /
Lauralee Farrer and Clayton J. Schmit

Includes bibliographical references.
1. Divine office—Liturgy. 2. Divine office—Music. 3. Psalmody. 4. Monastic and religious Life. I. Schmit, Clayton J. II. Title III. Series

CALL NUMBER BX2000.P85 2010
ISBN: 978-1-60899-278-2

PRAYING THE HOURS IN ORDINARY LIFE
Art for Faith's Sake 5

Cascade Books
An imprint of Wipf and Stock Publishers
199 W. 8th Ave., Suite 3
Eugene, OR 97401
www.wipfandstock.com

New Revised Standard Version Bible, copyright 1989, Division of Christian Education of the National Council of the Churches of Christ in the United States of America. Used by permission. All rights reserved. Note: Typographic and format changes have been made for ease of readability in liturgies.

Written by Lauralee Farrer and Clayton J. Schmit
Illustrations by Denise Louise Klitsie
Translations by Martina Nagel
Cover jacket design by Denise Louise Klitsie
Book design by Loren A. Roberts/Hearken Creative
LTC Garamont and FF Scala Sans were used for the book cover and chapter heads. Book copy was set in Type-Together's Athelas, FF Scala Sans, and Times New Roman.

 CASCADE *Books* • Eugene, Oregon

TABLE OF CONTENTS

TABLE OF ILLUSTRATIONS
by Denise Louise Klitsie

TABLE OF TRANSLATIONS
from Rainer Maria Rilke's *Book of Hours*
translations from the German by Martina Nagel

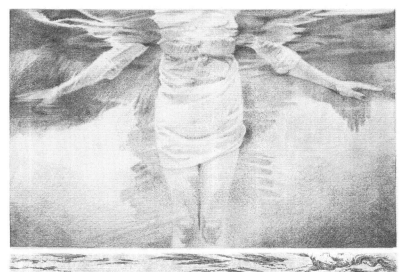

Stand at the crossroads and look;
ask for the ancient paths,
ask where the good way is, and walk in it,
and you will find rest for your souls.

—JEREMIAH 6:16

This book

is

for Marcie Schmit

who taught me to say my prayers

and to sing my faith

and

for Bette Farrer

who knew that to pray

is to love.

Hear my cry, O God,

Listen to my prayer.

—PSALM 61:1

ETERNITY IN OUR HEARTS

My life has not turned out the way I thought it was going to. Was ever a thought more startling or more universal? How curious it is that change surprises and threatens us even though it is so familiar, even though it happens in infinite layers upon itself, in every aspect of our lives.

Everything that is alive changes because everything that is alive *moves*. The ancient Greek philosopher Heraclitus framed it timelessly—no one ever steps in the same river twice, he said, for the river changes and so does the person. Yet even those of us who believe in a sovereign Creator persist in our dogged cycles of shock and resistance to change.

French impressionist Claude Monet found light rather than water to be the fluid variable that made it impossible for him to paint the same landscape twice. Monet was inspired by the moving light that forced him to constantly change his palette of colors. He was tyrannized by it, too, for the light would not stay still long enough for him to capture it on canvas.

God is the variable that changes the landscape of the lives of His followers, keeping us in tension between inspiration and tyranny. Ever the same, yet never predictable, God is alive. He *moves*. Even to our detriment, we ignore all the evidence to this: waking and sleeping, we lay waste our powers in the context of His omnipotence; agonize over the past and the future while in His present; squint in shock at life, knowing full well of His omniscience. The sun and the moon move like spotlights over creation, "See, here I am. And here. And here." We shade our eyes against Him, however, in stupor or rebellion, and plow through our days in our ignoring, until love or suffering (or both) snaps us out of it.

Never was this more evident to me than when I stuttered onto praying the divine Hours, during a season when my own were filled with grief, and I longed for the solace of a landscape to match my sorrow. A brief dream of a woman shading her eyes from the sun was enough to drive me desert-ward, and along the way, I stumbled on a quote from Thomas Merton that was the beginning of a path out of my uninhabitable life. He warned, "The logic of worldly success rests on a fallacy—the strange error that our perfec-tion depends on the thoughts and opinions and applause of other men! A weird life it is, indeed, to be living always in somebody else's imagina-tion, as if that were the only place in which one could at last become real."[1] It was the weird life that I chose to leave behind. Becoming real was the new destination.

Merton, unknown to me then, became the first point on the map of my journey. I was bold and stupid: I prayed ridiculous prayers that God answered gracefully, with a logic that communicated His presence to my fractured mind. I drove into Taos, New Mexico, one day and stopped at a bookstore that sold exclusively mystery paperbacks. I said, "I'm looking for anything by Thomas Merton and a book by St Augustine called *Confessions*." The proprietor did not say, "Lady, it's a mystery *paperback* bookstore." He just looked at me as though I was from the future, and gestured to a wall of books. The shelves were crammed with fiction, all bound at the same height and more or less the same depth. Between two three-inch thick, well-thumbed, broken-spined, paperback novels were two books of a different shape: Thomas Merton's *Wisdom of the Desert*, and St. Augustine's *Confessions*. I said, "those are the ones I'm looking for," bought them, and left as though I had ordered them in advance. I have to give it to God on this one: a bookstore devoted solely to mysteries.

I learned a little about the desert fathers from Merton, but what he really gave me was the idea of a monk in ordinary life.[2] Grief had driven me not outside myself, but deeper in than I knew I could stretch. Merton supplied my first hopeful thought: *Instead of vaporizing, maybe I could be a monk in ordinary life.*

I was in the desert for fifty days. Later, reflecting on those dates, I would discover they coincided with the liturgical season of Lent. I came from a Protestant tradition with no awareness of the liturgical calendar, of monastic vows, of ancient spiritual disciplines. I did not know what Advent was. When I discovered Merton, I thought he was as old as Athanasius of Alexandria. I had no idea that hermits and monastics still existed—much less that I was sleeping on top of my truck not far from Christ in the Desert monastery in Abiquiu. I had no idea what "divine Hours" were. The closest thing to ancient tradition in my church was anything made with lime jello. Yet, without knowing it, I was following in the footsteps of the father of Western monasticism.

Benedict, as a young man, left a life of privilege, sick in soul and in great turmoil of heart, and went into the desert to find God. Why should I be surprised to find similar evidences of Him, leading to similar daily prayers? I did what made sense to me—I prayed when the sun set and again before bed. I prayed in the wakeful, un-tranquil night and later when the dawn came. I prayed when I found the courage to rise from sleep, when the day began to disintegrate, when the sun burned overhead and in the lonely afternoons. My prayers at each of those different hours naturally matched the moods and emotions of them. Later, when I was to "discover" the Benedictine tradition of keeping the divine Hours, I should have been shocked at the coincidences, but I wasn't.

I did not know there was a name and a tradition for what I was doing, but this is really no more or less than saying I went into the desert and found God in the same way that others had before me. Why should that be surprising, when it is God's intention to be found? The story is told of Albert Schweitzer's visit to Equatorial Africa, where he talked with a tribal chief about God. The chief nodded in recognition at Schweitzer's story, saying "we knew someone passes on the edge of the forest, but we never knew his name."[3] God passed on the edges of my desert until I found Him. Simple as that.

During that season I lived from one hour to the next, marked not by the clock but by the changing light of day, with prayers to match. It sustained me until I regained my faculties. More than that, it recalibrated my own nature to the Nature around me. Living in God-made time saved my life. Later, as I began to reenter polite society, I never regained my confidence in man-made time any more than in the Easter Bunny. I can function in man-made time, of course—I can meet you at 1 p.m. on a Wednesday in May if you want. But I cannot ever fully go back, nor *would* I if given the option, any more than Lazarus would have returned to earth from heaven, except that the Master beckoned.

Since those difficult days, the maturing of my experience in praying the Hours has been as unpredictable and circuitous as my introduction was. The deeper I go, the more I experience the sensation of finding something I've lost in a place I've never been before. The mysteries of the Hours are now less difficult to believe than the thought that their personalities were ever hidden to me: how the morning light comes with joy; how in the late afternoon, when shadows lengthen, I am tempted to melancholy; how things happen at three in the morning that would never happen any other time of day.

At eight particular times of day the ancients stopped to remember God's presence, and to remember that the full complement of creation exists to describe Him to us. Each of the Hours has a distinct personality for recognizing part of the character of God. It's natural that two in the morning is different than two in the afternoon. The former is a *Vigils* Hour, dangerous, still, piercing, lonesome. The latter is *None*, when the slats of the window blinds slice up the light in a way that can, inexplicably, break your heart with yearning. Though this archaic way of naming the Hours is no longer common as it once was, even the most modern of us resonates with recognition: We all know bright, well-intentioned mornings; sleepy, coffee-spiked afternoons; re-luctant sundowns where disappointment finally gives way to rest; and nights both passionate and isolated. We have our own versions of "praying" those Hours. This, every human being does religiously because our bodies are tuned to it. The seasons of a year follow the same pattern as the Hours. As well, the seasons of a life. To discover this reverberated rhythm is to find a core that defines both the individual and the collective, powerful enough to bind us to each other as made in the image of God, in spite of our differences.

Observing the Hours of prayer is older even than Christ himself, reaching back through Jewish and Muslim religious observances, yes, but to my mind it began with Eden. God has surrounded us in nature (our own and the world around us) that resounds with His presence. His purpose is to be found, and nature's purpose is to show the way. And unlike the shallow surface of ordinary life that we have designed to continually remind us of the lives *we* have created, God's presence gets deeper, richer, fuller, wider, and more fecund the more you dive into it. I came to the divine Hours quite out of ignorance and suffering, which may explain my peculiar take on it, but the stream I found in the desert is as elemental as the Beginning itself.

This eternity, to which nature is a witness, is more than something that happens to us after we die. It is a great river flowing beneath the surface of everything else, in which we were meant to live and move and have our being. As the late theologian Ray Anderson reminded his students, "we are made of dust, yet we have eternity in our hearts."[4] Eden in our hearts—whether desert or forest or mountaintop—where we might walk again with God in the twilight of the day.

To pray the Hours is to engage with a living thing. Spoken into life at the Beginning, Benedict's rule hardened the bones of it, and years of monastic practice have toughened its muscles and sinew. Contemporary monastics Karl Rahner and David Steindl-Rast, the elegant Phyllis Tickle, and an increasing community of others enflesh the hours anew. The handful of artists whose work is reflected in this book respectfully hope to give another expression to its face. Our intention is to ponder the forgotten Eden, and how we might have forgotten even to *yearn* for it. To ask, *how can we learn to pray the Hours as if they were grace rather than spend them as if they were money?* How can the impossible charge to pray without ceasing be translated into a way of being rather than a burden of doing?

St. Bernard of Clairvaux said, "The soul must seek light by following the light." There are monasteries architecturally designed so that the Hours of prayer are marked by shadows cast in the buildings by the moon and the sun. This is what Lucien Hervé calls the "architecture of truth."[5] We ourselves are designed like these cathedrals, to reflect his glory in the changing shapes and shadows of our hours. This is multiplied exponentially with each unique life—one shaped to sing his glory, another to dance it, one to paint, one to speak, one to film, and another yet to invent forms that have not been invented yet, to evidence glory of God that is also new.

Our unorthodox breviary, *Praying the Hours in Ordinary Life,* is cousin to the long line of books containing public or canonical prayers, hymns, psalms, readings, and notations for everyday use. In it, we hope to bear witness to the Light of the World that Benedict so wisely suggested we stop eight times a day to acknowledge, and we owe acknowledgement to all those who have preceded us in doing so.

As with all testimonies to something too big for a single imagination, each generation, each individual story, brings a new contribution. If God is bigger than we are, and God is, and if each of us bears some small but complete spark of His divine image, as we do, then perhaps it is *because* our stories are inadequate that they must all be told. An eternity will be necessary to learn in detail each of the aspects we have to describe of God. But what if, by gathering those stories, one might hope to form little by little a vision of the One who is otherwise beyond our imagination? What glory that would be, to listen with leisure to God's story in all its infinite metamorphoses. This is an infinity that promises adventure and hope and epiphany and revelation in an unending stream. No wonder it is called heaven.

—*Lauralee Farrer*

St. Benedict

ST. BENEDICT AND THE LITTLE BLACK BIRD

Upon a certain day being alone, the tempter was at hand: for a little black bird, commonly called a merle or an ousel, began to fly about his face, and that so near as the holy man, if he would, might have taken it with his hand: but after he had blessed himself with the sign of the cross, the bird flew away: and forthwith the holy man was assaulted with such a terrible temptation of the flesh, as he never felt the like in all his life.

—Gregory the Great, *Dialogues* (1911) Book 2

HOW TO USE THIS BOOK

This resource for the Divine Office is intended to bring the experience of praying the Hours to communities that are largely unfamiliar with the practice and its deep spiritual value. It contains an introductory chapter on the nature of *kairos* time (Time is not Money) and one on the history of chant and fixed-hour prayer (Ceaseless Prayer, Endless Song). These are followed by a section that comprises the heart of this book: A series of essays by Lauralee Farrer on the personalities of each Hour of prayer, concluding with a poem by the German poet Rainer Maria Rilke and translated for this volume by Martina Nagel; then, the presentation of liturgies representing the offices of the *opus Dei*. The liturgies for these Hours have been compiled from historical and contemporary resources. They draw upon biblical and other texts typically associated with particular hours of prayer. Each of the eight liturgies is presented in a format that falls within the range of tradition associated with its office. The chant forms for the psalms are also traditional and hardly original. The original portions of the liturgies include some of the prayers and all of the cyclical chants that make up the Hour refrains. Here, the chant texts are by Lauralee and the melodies and musical arrangements have been composed by me. For those interested in bringing layers of variation to the music of the cyclical chants that comprise the Hour refrains, there is an appendix containing musical arrangements. Throughout the book, you will find original illustrations created for this volume by Denise Louise Klitsie.

Suggestions for Praying the Hours

It is common in many Christian traditions to pray portions of the Divine Office. Some congregations hold daily or weekly Matins (morning prayer) services or Vespers services. There is a strong tradition in Great Britain for cathedral choirs to sing Vespers each evening. Other Christians attend to the Divine Office while on retreats where it is convenient to set aside times of prayer during days of reflection. Even there, however, it is uncommon for Christians outside of monastic communities to pray the entire Office throughout a twenty-four hour period. There are also believers who commit themselves to fixed-hour prayer as a regular part of their daily devotion. Some of these elect to become oblates, lay persons associated with monastic communities who live out their spirituality within ordinary life. The commitment of oblates usually involves some fixed-hour prayer, prayed privately or with other believers who hold one another accountable to spiritual commitments. Praying the Divine Office, even in part, is a rich spiritual exercise that draws believers into an encounter with their Creator and creates resonance with Christians of all times who have submitted to the wisdom of the church by engaging in endless prayer and ceaseless song.

The collection of liturgies contained in *Praying the Hours in Ordinary Life* can be used as a template for prayer, either private or communal, and the Hours can be celebrated in part or in whole. There is a particular benefit, however, in seeing the full Divine Office as one unbroken line of prayer that, in spite of its inconvenience to modern lifestyles, brings spiritual renewal and meaning. As one ministry student said at the conclusion of an experience with the Hours in an intensive seminary class held at a monastery in Italy, "Praying the Hours was my most memorable experience from Orvieto—praying over a period of twenty-four hours, in a sacred and intentional space, has affected the way I view my spirituality and informed how I want to continue to relate to the Divine."[6] Most of us will not be able to pray the eight Hours every day or even regularly. The hope for this resource is that groups of believers will engage in occasional experiences with the Divine Office and to pray the full Office, with all its bother and benefit. Whether this occurs during retreats or as part of intensive community experiences (such as a course on spirituality), the authors hope to encourage those unfamiliar with these monastic practices to find the benefit of engaging in the

opus Dei in their own lives of faith.

Those wishing to enter into a twenty-four hour engagement with the Divine Office are encouraged to begin their prayer with Vespers. Monastic communities typically follow the Jewish custom of welcoming a new day at sundown. Vespers kindles a light to mark a new day in Christ.

Understanding Ritual

Monastic prayer is not intended to be "high liturgy." Nor does it settle for the lowest common denominator of liturgical taste, with its aversion to ritual and its tendency toward casualness and chatter. The Divine Office is prayed by persons who understand that ritual is a crucial part of everyday life. Each of us has private rituals for rising, grooming, eating, working, and retiring at night. We have public rituals for sporting events like singing the national anthem or "Take Me Out to the Ball Game." We practice rituals that govern our behavior at civic meetings, parades, holiday celebrations, and so forth. Praying the Hours is a call to submit to the ritual way of life. Some Christians will say that they avoid rituals in worship because they don't want their adoration to become rote and wooden. While many of us have seen instances where ritual and dullness have seemed synonymous, such an observation is indicative of two misconceptions.

The first misconception is that ritual and inspiration are incompatible. The Holy Spirit has used the rituals of meal, prayer, song, and worship from the beginning of faith. In them is found the Bread of Life and Living Water. Through them come an awareness of God's presence and resonance with God's people.

The second misconception is that "low worship" is without ritual and liturgy. A remark once shared by a Pentecostal pastor makes the point: "My church doesn't have a liturgy. Of course, we worship in the same way, with the same order every week. If I ever tried to change the order of worship, I would need to look for a new job." In other words, all churches have liturgies, whether "high" or "low."

Our liturgical rituals define us as communities of faith and ought to be owned, acknowledged, and celebrated. The Hours are simple liturgies built of quiet ritual practices. Those who lead in their celebration are advised to avoid the temptation of making them more elaborate than necessary or more plain than is effectual.

In worship we acknowledge that there are rituals that have the power to do more than regulate our activities and comportment. They have what Graham Hughes calls an iconic quality. The rituals of worship bring us to the border of the knowable world, to that place where we can "imagine how things are in the presence of God."[7] Accordingly, in praying the Hours, we allow the simple ritual forms of prayer and song to speak for us and to speak on their own. We avoid overlaying them with verbal explanations and directions. They are intended to be executed with generous simplicity and measures of silence.

There is always a need for a few persons to be appointed to plan worship for the gathering of God's people. The offices in this book call for one or a few people to learn the chant melodies and to lead the prayers. Some of the liturgies call for "One" who will preside by saying a greeting or benediction. This person should be named in advance of each liturgy and possess the grace to know when to proffer gentle leadership. Others will be appointed to read lessons or offer prayers. One of the scriptural values of the Hours is the shared "priesthood of all believers." Any willing person can assume leadership for a portion of each liturgy. Clergy typically serve in roles of worship leadership; here, they are neither necessary nor excluded. Let the leaders know their parts and rehearse them so that when the time for prayer comes, the office can be sung by all

with subtle direction, but certain guidance.

Insofar as possible, try to avoid giving directions throughout each office. The liturgies are presented on the page in such a way that they need no announcements or instructions. Extraneous talk has the power to stifle, even suffocate ritual practices. On their own, rituals are multivalent, meaning many things to many people, allowing for all meanings to coexist and to be equally valid. To explain a ritual or a symbol is to reduce its meaning to merely one thing. The contemplation of mystery is not aided by interruption. Let this encouragement be given one last time: *Resist, resist, resist*, the temptation to clutter the rituals with talk. *Embrace, embrace, embrace* their power to reorient your noisy world to God.

The songs and chants in these liturgies are simple and attainable by average singers; they require little or no advance group rehearsal. Confident musical guidance will result from leaders who prepare carefully so that the assembly can perform their parts with minimal practice. If time allows, it may be useful to your community to rehearse the chanting of the psalms and the singing of the cyclical chants before it enters the first Hour of prayer. Directions for learning to lead the chants follow below.

Above all, let each office be bathed in silence. These are the times where the soul is trained to listen for that still small voice of God that can only be heard at the iconic frontier where we tread delicately toward the edge of mystery.

The Prayers

Each of the offices has a time appointed for corporate prayer. The form of prayer may vary. A few suggestions follow as to how leaders might shape the corporate prayers. Before we consider the forms, a few words of advice will guide the prayer leaders in their planning.

First, remember that as you lead the people in prayer, you are encouraging their participation. When you pray aloud in their behalf, let your prayers be statements to which they can give assent. Their expected response is "Amen." It means they agree with all you have said for them. Avoid using language that is overly colloquial, lest the people not understand you. Avoid statements charged with opinion, lest they disagree with you. Prayer leaders may hold strong opinions but need to set them aside as they submit themselves to serve the concerns of those gathered.

Second, be aware that prayers in public worship are spoken to God and not to the people. The self-evidence of this statement is absurdly apparent, yet in public worship we regularly hear prayer leaders speaking in ways that chide worshipers ("Open their pocketbooks, O God, so that they will be generous when the offering is taken today") or pepper our petitions with announcements ("We pray for Helen, who is in room 617 at Memorial hospital and eager to receive visitors"). Prayers address God. There are other times to address the people.

Third, let the language of prayer be suitable for public use. Intimate language and personal disclosure can be embarrassing to witness and do not call forth the Amen of the people.

The forms suitable for public prayers during the office are many and can change from service to service. The bidding prayer is effective. Here, the leader guides prayer with suggestions ("I ask your prayers for all who are alone this night," etc.) and the assembly responds by praying in silence. In this form, numerous "bids" are typically offered by the leader. Another useful form is for the leader to offer petitions, each of which ends formulaically. The assembly responds with a fixed affirmation (One: "We pray for peace. God in your mercy," All: "Hear our prayer").

The ancient form of prayer known as the *collect* (pronounced \'**kä**-likt) is a form particularly fitting for prayers during the offices. Its pattern fits well the ritual environment of the Hours. The collect (so named because it collects worship themes into one prayer) has this five-part structure: 1) address to God, 2) statement about God, 3) petition(s), 4) purpose, and 5) closure. Many written collects have a formal, "high liturgy" tone. However, with careful language selection, they can also be composed with ordinary and meaningful speech. Here is an example fitting for Vespers:

1) God of Light, 2) you gave us Jesus as the Light of the World. 3) Let His light shine among us this evening 4) so that we can see His glory and reflect it in our lives. 5) We pray in His name, Amen.

Extemporized prayers can also be used. When offered by persons with natural gifts for poetic expression, their artistry can draw the community into contemplation and assent.

Prayer leadership may be shared with the entire praying community. Those offering prayers and petitions for each office should be selected in advance to give them time to prepare. Even extempore speakers need time to prepare their thoughts, if not their exact speech. Rather than selecting prayers from published sources, it is recommended that leaders craft original prayers fitting to the concerns of the immediate community and suitable to the Hour. The prayers can be comprised of several collects or petitions or many bids. A number of people can share in leading the prayers. Let there be silence between each petition.

A final comment regarding the Lord's Prayer, which is common to all the Hours. It should be voiced aloud by the entire assembly. The prayer is introduced in a plain manner. It may be announced: "The Lord's Prayer," although this is redundant given that it is clearly indicated in the order of service. Alternatively, the leader can begin without an announcement by speaking the opening phrase; the community will understand that it is expected to join in. It matters little which version of The Lord's Prayer is used. It should be one with which the community is familiar. Note that if a leader desires to lead in a contemporary voicing of the prayer that begins with "Our Father in heaven, . . ." she should be sure to lead by confidently speaking the entire phrase. Invariably, if a leader begins by pausing after the second word ("Our Father, . . .") the community will see the pause as a signal to recite the traditional version (". . . which art in heaven.")

Chanting the Psalms

The psalms in this version of the Divine Office, along with their responses (the *Gloria*

Patri or *Gloria in Excelsis*), are to be chanted by all in the assembly. They are sung in unison, either by everyone at once or antiphonally.

Antiphonal singing calls for one group (or one side of the assembly) to sing the first part of a verse and another group (or side) to sing the remainder of the verse. Groupings may be suggested by a worship leader: for example, adults alternating with children, students with teachers, those seated on the right side with those on the left, those seated in an inner circle of chairs with those in an outer circle. Let a worship leader give a simple direction to all indicating the group designations for singing the psalm. Antiphonal chanting is indicated where the psalm verses are divided and marked with these symbols: † and ‡.

The psalms appointed for antiphonal singing in this book are all to be sung together on a single pitch (there is no harmony). The leader need only to begin the first (†) group by selecting a pitch and starting to sing. The members of the first group will naturally follow. The second (‡) group will respond, singing the remainder of each verse on the same tone. The pattern continues throughout the psalm as well as through the *Gloria Patri* or the *Gloria in Excelsis*.

An antiphonal psalm sung on a single tone:

†Sing to the Lord with thanksgiving; make melody to our God on the lyre.

‡He covers the heavens with clouds, prepares rain for the earth, makes grass grow on the hills.

There are many traditional ways to chant the psalms. Only two additional forms are presented in this version of the Divine Office. Both of them derive from the straightforward practice of chanting the text on a single tone.

The first psalm melody calls for unison singing throughout the psalm. It has a simple shape. It begins on a single pitch (selected by the psalm leader). The text is sung on that pitch until near the end of a verse where the pitch descends a full step for a few syllables of text, and then returns to finish the verse on the original pitch. The point of descent is marked in the text by a downward slash (\), while the point of return to the original pitch is marked by an upward slash (/).

A psalm sung with a simple melody:

Protect me, O God,   for in you I \ take / refuge.

The second psalm melody, though easy to sing, is slightly more involved than the first in that it has two parts. Again, it calls for all to sing the entire psalm (and appointed response) in unison. Each verse begins with a single pitch upon which the first phrase is sung. Near the end of the first half of the verse, an upward slash (/) indicates that the pitch rises a full step. The second half of the verse begins with an asterisk (*) indicating a return to the original pitch. Near the end of the second half of each verse, the pitch descends (\) a full step for a few syllables and returns again to the original pitch (/) to complete the verse.

A psalm sung on a melody with two parts:

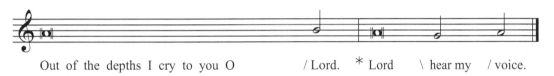

Out of the depths I cry to you O   / Lord.   * Lord   \ hear my   / voice.

Communities completely unfamiliar with psalm chanting may want to practice together in advance of praying the Hours in order to learn the rudiments of this simple art.

The Cyclical Chants

Each of the liturgies in this book contains a refrain (the Vespers Refrain, the None Refrain, etc.). The refrains are intended to be sung near the beginning of each Hour and repeated (as indicated in the order of service) at intervals during each office. They serve as a melodic refrain that provides identity and suggests personality for each office.

The refrains are Taizé style chants that follow a "theme and variations" form (see the description of Taizé music in the chapter "Ceaseless Prayer, Endless Song"). While having some similarity to Gregorian Chant, they do not require monastic training. They are designed to be sung by lay people with average musical ability. Like plain chant, they create the musical potential of drawing participants into contemplation in a way that mere speaking cannot accomplish. Worship has always been resplendent with music because of its particular powers to accompany texts, allowing their words to penetrate the veil of the ineffable and speak to things that are too deep for words. Cyclical chants exercise this capacity of sung prayer. Each time they are sung within an office, they are voiced repeatedly, allowing for added layers of resonance to form as people sing the printed harmonies, improvise others, and hear the melodic variations supplied in the music appendix. There is no prescribed number of times a chant should be sung. Each iteration of it within a service will find its natural ending

place, whether it has been sung thrice or a dozen times. Even as each of the Hours is prayed without hurry, the refrains can take their time and determine their own proper space. They are created to exist in *kairos* time (see "Time Is Not Money" for an explanation of this term).

Accomplished musicians will face the temptation of adding musical accompaniment and instrumentation to the cyclical chants. Yet, the humble nature of praying the Hours dictates that the chants be sung in a plain manner with simple harmonization, if any at all. Guitar chords are provided in the musical arrangements. If used, they should provide quiet strummed or plucked accompaniment. An instrument in the key of C, such as a recorder, flute, violin, or oboe, can play any or all of the *obbligato* variations (found in the music appendix) as the chants are sung. If more than one instrument is available, the variations can be played as duets, selecting from them in any order. It is the vocal inventing of harmonies and the instrumental variations that keep the repeated melodic theme from becoming dull. As Tom F. Driver has observed, there is a difference between monotony and boredom. "Liturgy is a full emptiness, a monotony without boredom, a reverent waiting without expectation."[8] Rituals are monotonous activities. They are repetitive and do not require concentration. What may appear as rote observance to an outsider is often experienced by participants as an activity that frees the mind and body for creative thought and expressive movement. In a world of constant commotion and demand, ritual monotony is a welcome relief. It can be found eight times a day for those who submit to the ceremonies of the *opus Dei*.

As the offices unfold, it will be useful for a recorder or other instrument to introduce a cyclical refrain by playing it through a single time. This will instruct the participants who will then join in with leaders as they sing the melodies. The instrumentalist may continue to play the melody a few times until the community is singing along reliably. At that point, harmonies and instrumental variations can be added.

How to Use These Liturgies When Praying the Hours on Successive Days

In the strictest tradition, monastic communities gather for prayer eight times a day, every day. Within a week, they pray through the entire Psalter. At the end of the liturgy included with each chapter on the Hours you will find psalm suggestions for communities desiring to use these liturgies in praying the Divine Office upon successive days. By tradition, psalms have been appointed for use during certain Hours. For example, Psalm 141, with its vivid petition, "Let my prayer rise before you as incense," has typically been appointed for use during Vespers. Some of the psalms lend themselves for use in more than one of the Hours of prayer.

Other Readings: While the psalms are the traditional heart of the *opus Dei* liturgies, other readings from Scripture and spiritual or devotional writers are usually included. When using these liturgies to pray the Divine Office on successive days, leaders are free to select other scriptural and spiritual readings that are suitable to the personality of each Hour and fitting for the season or occasion of prayer.

How to Prepare a Holy Space for Prayer

When monastics pray the *opus Dei*, they typically have chapels available for quiet, contemplative prayer. Finding such spaces in ordinary life may be difficult. Some churches have small chapels that are suitable. Retreat centers, often established by monastic communities, are situated throughout North America and are welcoming sites for those desiring to pray. The chants in these liturgies will sound fine in nearly any quiet setting. However, if a resonant space can be used, the sound of reverberating chant will bring about a subtle value: resonance with and reminiscence of ancient brothers and sisters in faith who once prayed the Hours in spaces made of hewn stone. Even softly sung prayers are enlarged with holy volume when they resound in a lively space.

Regardless of the worship site available to you, certain things can be done to reverence the space for prayer. Candles are especially appropriate at Vespers, where we reflect on Christ, the Light of the World. They are also preferable to incandescent lighting during the night time Hours. Lighting should not be bright, yet sufficient candlelight is needed to allow for people to read the liturgies. Members of each praying community may volunteer to serve their friends by arriving early to light the candles, situate a cross and other worship symbols, and make arrangements for seating. In cold climes, they might even kindle a fire for warmth in advance of the community's arrival. (For an example of how this might be done, see "A Holy Space," which follows this chapter.)

If the seating in your worship space is flexible, it can be placed in creative configurations. Chairs can be set in a circle, or in concentric circles; they can be situated in two groups facing one another across centrally placed symbols (such as a cross and a Christ candle), or four groups facing inward toward the center. When the chants and readings are divided between two groups, the configuration of the chairs can provide a point for settling group designations (for example, right side and left side, or inner circle and outer circle, etc.). The liturgies have a subtle marking (Ω) to indicate fitting occasions to kneel for prayer. Where possible, allow enough space between rows of chairs for people to slip into a kneeling posture at the indicated times. In some worship settings, pews are equipped with kneelers. Where none are available, it is ap- propriate for worshipers who are able to kneel directly on the floor.

When praying the daylight Hours, your community may find it convenient to pause for prayer in work places, even out of doors. Gathering for prayer in a garden, or under a shady tree can be a refreshing respite from the day's activities.

—*Clay Schmit*

In 2008, at an intensive class in Orvieto, Italy, students and faculty added to their study a twenty-four-hour period of praying through the Hours while residing in an ancient monastery. It was so powerful an experience that it was repeated the following year, when Nate Risdon led the group. We are indebted to Nate for recording his thoughts on creating a holy space for praying the Hours, and for giving us permission to include it here in its entirety.

—*Clay Schmit*
Lauralee Farrer

A HOLY SPACE

*"It is space on earth that is made holy, not because of the place itself
but because of what God does for humans in that place."*

JAMES F. WHITE

One of the essential elements to consider when praying the Hours, whether you gather in community or pray alone, is the place in which you pray. Thinking with intention about the space will help you to see place as a gift—as a place "set-aside," as a "sacred" space—rather than as an ordinary, utilitarian space.

This intention can also aid you in stepping out of ordinary time and into *kairos* time where God longs to meet us. Such purposeful thinking about holy space is not new. It is in keeping with a long tradition of the use of space in worship dating back to the elaborate and detailed instructions given to the Israelites for building the Temple in Jerusalem, as found in 1 Kings and 1 Chronicles. This intention was reflected by the early church as worship moved into basilica and with the building of cathedrals. Jesus had holy space in mind when he said:

> The hour is coming when you will worship the Father neither on this mountain nor in Jerusalem. . . . But the hour is coming, and is now here, when the true worshippers will worship the Father in spirit and truth. (John 4:21, 23a)

With these words, Jesus was giving divine approval to the idea that sacred space was no longer centralized in one area of one temple in one city; it could be found anywhere in God's creation. This was certainly a comfort to the Samaritan woman at the well, who represented a people long ignored by much of the culture around them. The Samaritans, and the space they inhabited, were under God's grace and purview.

Decades later, the dispersed Jews that were part of the early church living throughout the Roman Empire found great comfort in these words. Travel was dangerous in many parts of the empire and a pilgrimage to Jerusalem was not to be undertaken lightly. They learned to establish sacred spaces in houses and secret places where they could worship in security.

Jesus' words can bring that same comfort for people around the world today. They may comfort the woman who cannot travel to a house of worship for fear that she will be jailed or killed by government officials. For her, sacred space might be the corner of her one-bedroom flat where a small icon of St. Nicholas gazes down upon her. God will meet her there. Jesus' words may comfort the man who might have to live out the rest of his life in isolation as a political prisoner. For him, sacred space might be a little patch of floor lit by the sun for two hours each day. God will meet him there. They may comfort the single father working sixteen-hour days in order to support his young children. For him, sacred space might be found during one thirty-minute meal break when he can gaze out a factory window to watch clouds pushed by the wind. God will meet him there.

We can apply Jesus' words about worshipping God in spirit and in truth to our own circumstances and the situations that make up the *chronos*, that is, the ordinary times in our lives. Perhaps sacred space is found by praying the Hours behind the wheel of your car as you inch through the traffic of your morning commute. God will meet you there.

Even there, we can take time to reinterpret, to re-imagine the space for prayer. Your car is no longer just a metal box with switches and gears controlled by the human hand. It is a space overflowing with the presence of the Spirit of God, the very One who moved over the face of the waters at the earth's inception. Wherever you pray, you can envision that space as sacred. As Jim White said, "It is space on earth that is made holy, not because of the place itself but because of what God does for humans in that place."[9] This can certainly be true for locations that we view as ordinary. A common

place is transformed in times of worship because of what God does there for us.

If you prayer the Hours in community, you may find that you have the opportunity to adjust an ordinary space to increase its suitability for corporate prayer. You might pray over the space and prepare it so that as people gather, they enter into a welcoming place. You might arrange the seating so as to center people for prayer. Preparing a place for prayer is a service to the community; it is also a spiritual exercise in itself. It takes into account the comfort of the people and their needs as worshipers. It also takes into account the intentions of the various Hours. Can the relocation of chairs allow for less distraction and more focus? Might a circular configuration of seating around a single candle serve the Vesper prayers? Might another configuration be fitting for Vigils where the prayers call for us to confront the darkness and the unknown?

If the space you use for praying the Hours can

be employed throughout the day and night, consider modifying it for each of the Hours. As an example, I recently led a group of students through an exercise of praying the Hours at an ancient monastery located on a hilltop in the town of Orvieto, Italy. The room we used was bare except for two wonderful triptychs on the north and south walls of the room, a few scattered chairs, and a table that served as a makeshift altar. As we readied ourselves for praying the Hours, I asked a small group of students to read through the essays and the Rilke poems included in this book. Then, I asked them to re-imagine the worship space that we would be using. The group set off to a local café and discussed the possibilities for nearly four hours. My original intention had been to have them set up the space before the first Hour and leave it in that state; however, the group re-envisioned the space in light of the personalities of each liturgy. They thoughtfully weighed how God might approach us differently, depending on

the Hour in which we were praying. The students made a careful and distinct floor plan for every Hour of prayer; each was dramatically different the others. Then, they volunteered to reset the worship space before each gathering. In setting the room, the team used things found in the closets and rooms of the monastery: a small collection of rocks, tea candles, lamps borrowed from the monastic cells, tables, and chairs, as needed. (During one hour of prayer, the assembly stood for the entire liturgy.)

When the community walked into the room for each liturgy, we found it changed every time. The changes had a profound influence on our times of prayer. We were unable to settle into a routine. Each time we had to negotiate our way into a new setting and find a place to settle down for prayer. The affect was amazing. Resetting the space each time opened our hearts to experience the mysteries of each Hour. Each reconfiguration of the space created a new awareness of what God was doing with us in that place and in that time. These simple, thoughtful gifts of hospitality by a few students became a means by which the entire assembly entered into *kairos*, God's time, and into His space. And He met us there.

—*Nate Risdon*

TIME IS NOT MONEY

I was standing in the deep doorway outside a shop in Boston avoiding the rain the first time I first saw someone throw away a handful of pennies. Picture the sort of doorway used by filmmakers as places where drugs or money or dignity are stolen in bad neighborhoods; where kisses are stolen in *You've Got Mail* movies; and where, in Jane Austen novels, soulful young Englishmen, born below the station of all the lovely young women, shiver in their inadequate topcoats.

A man exited the shop and threw a handful of pennies to the gutter of the cobblestoned street. Presumably he was already carrying as much weight as he could bear. Most of the coins flew to the gutter as though they knew themselves to be of no more worth than the 97% zinc that the penny has become, a sad reflection of its former copper glory. The stoic face of Lincoln flew in a dozen spinning directions. I would like to say that one of those pennies circled and circled in slow motion before it stopped. That, like Cool Hand Luke, it did not lay down willingly—that it did not splash gently into that dark mud. It did not *actually* happen; even so, in my imagination I saw the face of Lincoln wheel round, upside down and right again until it came to a wobbly rest, and I thought, *what a miracle a penny is.*

I saw men and clever machines mining zinc from natural mineral deposits of ore in the earth's crust, possibly as far away as China. This was mixed with a tiny amount of copper, squeezed from an eyedropper designed by Willy Wonka, and hand-pressed by a thousand identical Oompa Loompas into discs crammed with arcane historical and metaphoric information. I woke in that Boston doorjamb just as one ambitious soccer mom in my imagination was sniffing rinsed plastic milk jugs where her high school sophomore daughter would collect 6,100 coins for charity at a weight of 34 pounds per jug.

A man threw away a handful of pennies, and the crust of the earth broke and I fell through to ancient Galilee and then to contemporary China and to Willy Wonka's chocolate factory and then to suburbia and back again in the time it took for those pennies to come to stasis. Back into reality came the choir of Lincolns facing upward in the rain or downward in the gutter. Fallen on hard times, beloved Abe who carried more on his narrow Kentuckian frame than should be required of one man. That sudden, vivid thought stole my breath and tears sprang to my eyes. My imagination, too, came then to rest because its work was done. It connected me.

The man who threw the handful of Abe onto the wet street did not weigh metaphor and meaning. He knows pennies are only worth what they can be traded for, and they are not worth carrying around all day where they will only stretch the fabric of his expensive slacks.

I do not blame him. Who stops to ponder what hands a penny may have passed through in its 30-year lifespan? Money's value is not sentimental, or poetic, or existential. It's cumulative: the disposal of a handful of pennies is a weight loss. The loss of a few dollars can sting, but not so much more than a spilled cappuccino. To risk hundreds of dollars is a sober enterprise, but to lose millions—that is what it takes to become tragic. That's enough to push a man from the multi-story skyscraping office to which those millions lifted him in the first place. So. Money is about value that is incremental, and to love it for itself, as many do, is to uncover the roots of all evil.

How we value money is both related to and symbolic of the dangerous way we value time—as a commodity that has cumulative value. Think of all the financial language we apply to time: waste time, buy time, lose time, spend time. As though it were something to be bartered with—as if, once spent, it might be gotten back again. We treat seconds like pennies in our pockets, routinely devalued. Hours can acceptably be wasted on learning who America's next top model is going to be—allowable losses in exchange for spending a tired evening in front of 500 cable channels. But what is that really? *Killing* time. No wonder that afterward we feel vaguely like killing ourselves. Maybe there's no difference, since we are speaking of increments.

Lost years are harder to ignore. Anyone killed in a car accident is a sad thing, but if that someone is 16 and just got her driver's license, that's tragic. Visit the children's hospital. It is especially difficult, why? Because they are so young. What you learn in those moments is that time is not something that you can earn back. It is not to be wasted, spent, lost, bought, or killed. Time is not money.

Kairos, the Uncounted Moment

We have a beginning and an end. We measure the span of our lives into digestible portions, and we wear little machines on our wrists that remind us of exactly how much is left in the account of each day. The clock is a man-made idea, clever, necessary, and entirely artificial. It is our Frankenstein; we have invented it, and now it tyrannizes us. The Greeks had a name for this clock time *and* for the tyranny it causes—they called it the god *Chronos*.

Father time. Goya painted this father as a monster eating his own children. Horrible, horrible.

We have to be taught *chronos*, because it is not organic. We learn it like the alphabet—by rote and repetition. One on the clock. Two o' the clock. Three o'clock. Endless numbered days, as Sam Beam says.[10] What is the time? Three. How much for the coffee? Two. This is the economy in which we "spend" our nine-to-fives, as if hours were currency, as if time were money. It's a system, intended to insure productivity, but it is without essence. You have only to imagine saying "be there Tuesday at seven" to a bushman, to a castaway, to a child-raised-by-wolves, to see how arbitrary it is, and how it actually diminishes the divine life of our hours. Controlling time by breaking it up into infinite little shards is akin to learning about the life of an exotic African animal by killing and autopsying it. Still, we march on to the beat of *chronos* and its tiny little whirring gears, its ticking drum.

There is another kind of time that the Greeks also named. *Kairos.* While *chronos* refers to chronological or sequential time, man-made time, *kairos* signifies a time in-between, an uncounted moment in which something outside of *chronos* happens. This time has God's image all over it, and belongs to Him. In the New Testament, *kairos* is used when referring to the moment that fulfills the purpose of God, the moment when God acts. Theologian Paul Tillich wrote of the *kairoi* as the crucial moments in history which change everything—the coming of Christ being the prime example.[11] While *chronos* is quantitative, *kairos* has a qualitative nature. But it does not require a world event to slip into *kairos*, really—ordinary life is full of movement between the two. It is within our power to slam shut the door between the two worlds or to move intentionally between them. We can enter the sacred space of *kairos* remarkably easily, in the way God made us to—through prayer.

Phyllis Tickle describes this in a global, communal context, that she found amazing: "the prayers I was offering were the same ones being offered by thousands of Christians in my time zone at exactly the same time I was offering them, as if we were indeed a cloud of witnesses and a great company of believers; amazing that the prayers I was offering were in large part the same prayers of praise and worship that my Lord had prayed and offered; amazing that increasingly as I prayed I could hear, as one friend of mine now says, 'a thousand's thousand voices' joining mine across all that is or has been or will be," she says.[12]

Ever constant, ever changing—the only way St. Benedict could imagine keeping up with the abundance of God's ongoing creation was to pray without ceasing—a state of being as much as a state of doing. This is one of the reasons why it is impossible to live the Christian life fully while maintaining one's own agenda. Who's got the time for anything more than staying engaged with what God is doing next? That's why Benedict stopped eight times a day to pray. (And, for a little bit of irony: who invented the mechanical clock by which we count the hours of *chronos* but the Benedictines! They did it in order to mark the time every day to pray the Hours.)

To Pray the Hours as If They Were Grace Rather than Spend Them as If They Were Money

You steal into a café for a quick break between two frantic portions of your day. It's three in the afternoon. The time of day that Christ died on the cross. You're yearning for something, though you don't know what. Something unlikely to be listed on a blackboard menu. You wonder briefly if anyone else feels this undifferentiated yearning. Something catches your attention—some Paul Simon tune, the way the sunlight moves on the floor lengthening the shadows, the earthy smell of espresso—and a trapdoor opens to the world that runs below the surface of your life. You fall through. Two seconds pass between that moment and when the barista starts snapping his fingers in your face, but you wake up a lifetime later. This sort of thing also happens in the deep doorways outside shops in Boston, in huge wooden wardrobes, in museum paintings and looking glasses—portals, all of them, to *kairos*.

Any big emotion can fracture time and open a portal. Love, for example. Even the possibility of love. Someone is supposed to drop by the house tonight—did ever an afternoon pass more slowly? Does time ever disappear so completely as when kissing is involved?

You've received a phone call, the one you have dreaded all your life whether you know it or not. It's your son hit by a car. It's your father with a heart attack. It's your doctor with the mammogram reports.

Through a strange fog that has filled your kitchen, your husband is saying something about how he never meant to hurt you—that he has always admired you, and wants you to be happy. Time stops. Next thing you know you are looking at the familiar clock in your familiar den, and it has melted like a Salvador Dali painting, and you have grown visibly older. You looked at that clock just a second ago and it was Tuesday. No, that doesn't make sense. You've been sitting here for hours now, and the clock hasn't even moved.

There are forty-eight minutes to wait until you can take pain medication again. You called the tow truck hours ago. Your six-month-old has been crying for six years straight. Is that possible?

What happens to you during these times? Where do you go when you are outside the reach of counted time? Each of us is given a portion of life, whether twenty-seven years or eighty-three, and we spend most of it governed by the artificial and the urgent, missing what is essential. Yet we are surrounded by things that have the power to take us beyond ourselves into the flow of a very different kind of time—the time that moves like a great river beneath even the most mundane of days. The Greek word for this time also means "grace."

When something potent—like love, or suffering—fractures your life, *chronos* cannot bear the weight of you anymore. Like Alice through the looking glass, you give way into someplace else. If you fall into *kairos*, and God grant that you will, the life you will find there is more real than real, more true than ordinary life. Is it possible to live in *kairos* instead of *chronos*, without opting out of society and joining a monastic order? Can we learn to stop wasting the hours and start praying them?

Here is part of the hidden nature of these two times: *chronos* is about boredom, about sameness, about stripping things of their individuality and conforming them to the ticking of a clock. It's *kairos* that is about ongoing creation. Surprising, isn't it? We think of it as the opposite—as though the clock is always changing and eternity is this great curse of a static future. Admit it—eternal life

sounds boring. We have a hard time imagining it through the filter of *chronos*. It's all sameness in this life and then fire and pain and back exercises in the hereafter if you fail. And if you do well, it's a choir of "holy holy holy" for infinity.

No wonder artists, who have less tolerance for the mundane, live lives that appear on the surface to be robust and sometimes debauched. Is it possible that we are searching for those portals into the eternal where we sense something of that mystery happening—whether substance induced, or physical intimacy, or any number of other possible paths to things that hint at transcendence. How many of us have destroyed ourselves on the shoals of that search, only to be offered no viable alternatives by the church—when it is union with God that we are searching for?

When we broke fellowship with God in Eden, an artificial end to our days known as "death" threw us out of harmony with this eternity in which we were created to live and breathe and have our being. We were snapped suddenly and irrevocably out of *kairos*, banished to the surface, into *chronos*, unable but for a few moments here and there to return—long enough to remember and to yearn. What if we are still surrounded by this Eden somehow, just under the surface of ordinary life? To grasp this is for the meaning of time to come into sudden clarity. Might we, like Eve, still walk with Him and talk with Him while He tells us we are His own? The beauty of eternity is communion with God—that's what was lost in the Garden and recovered on the cross. Does the God of *Kairos* truly offer eternal life, because He so loved us, in exchange for the Father *Chronos* who devours His children?

Eugene Peterson says that what God did at creation He did not finish in Genesis, but He is still doing now. Still creating the garden. He says that our exile is without form and void just as the cosmos was, and that God still hovers over the face of our waters. Paraphrasing Isaiah, Peterson says, "Did you think creation was over and done with when the mountains were carved, the rivers set flowing, and the Lebanon cedars planted? Did you think that salvation is only a date in the history books and some stories you heard from your grandparents? The Creator is still creating, here in Babylon!"[13] The savior is still saving, here in our time.

We often come to knowledge of praying the Hours at a time in life when things came to an end that we think can have no end, when things are lost that we think are required to sustain life, and yet we live—whether we want to or not. Falling through the crust of *chronos*, we are caught by something deeper, wilder, more unpredictable, and more powerful. Not a wristwatch to remind us of how much time is lost, or how little is left, but a God who still walks at the edge of the garden, and who always Is, right now and right now and right now.

—*Lauralee Farrer*

CEASELESS PRAYER, ENDLESS SONG

What would the ancients have seen? What would they have heard? How would they have prayed? Our mothers and fathers in faith, even from pre-Christian days, would have known and practiced ceaseless prayer and endless song. They would have heard pious Jews praying throughout the day, both in spontaneous blessings and at prescribed times of prayer. They would have heard the tolling of Roman public bells to announce the times of the workday. They would have used the sound of city bells to remind them it was time to pray. And, our forebears would have heard singing. The chanting of psalms was as familiar to Jesus and Paul and other devout Jews as it later was (and is) to monastic communities. At set hours of prayer and at other moments of devotion, the pious Jew and early Christian would sing psalms as well as hymns of faith. The life of the devout person was marked by unending cycles of prayer and song.

When the apostle Paul advises believers to pray without ceasing in his letters, he is not inventing a new devotional practice. Nor is he imposing an impossible task on his followers. Clearly, no person could pray with every breath.

He is merely encouraging the continuation of a common practice derived from Jewish observances long before his time. Not only was it common for the religious Jew to cease from ordinary activities during the work week to pray at least three times during the day—in the morning, at midday, and in the evening—the most pious believers would offer blessings up to a hundred times a day. The ancient rabbis crafted prayers to cover nearly every contingency in ordinary life. Thus, a scrupulous Jew such as Paul—like Jesus before him—probably offered a blessing each time he washed, or dressed, or drank a sip of water. Certainly, he would have offered a blessing before and after every meal and a separate blessing before enjoying a cup of wine. When a faithful person beheld a stunning sunset, there was a blessing for that. The blessings followed a familiar pattern known as the *berakhah*. Each began with the phrase: "Blessed are you, O God, King of the universe . . ." and would conclude with the appropriate clause: ". . . who has created the fruit of the vine" before a cup of wine, or "who bestows benefits upon the undeserving," upon being rescued from danger. To this day, the *berakhah* is among the most familiar phrases heard upon the lips of religious Jews.

To pray without ceasing kept (and keeps) a believer constantly in mind of God's presence and providence. It also bestowed upon the whole of one's existence an aura of holiness. A person could hardly be voicing God's praise throughout the day with sincerity while conniving to cheat in business or take advantage of a neighbor. When a person's mind is on God so continuously, it does seem as if every breath becomes a prayer of gratitude for life and for all that the eyes of faith behold.

While the regimen of blessings occupied the mind and lips of devout Jews dozens of times a day, the faithful would also engage in at least three particular periods of prayer, following the pattern of Daniel ("who got upon his knees three times a day," Daniel 6:11) and Psalm 55:17 ("evening and morning and noon I utter my complaint and moan, and he will hear my voice.") Formal times of daily prayer were held in local synagogues where psalms were sung and prayers were said in various forms. Though Paul and his contemporaries had no wrist watches to alert them as to when services would begin, the times would not be difficult to determine. The ever-efficient Romans, who governed Palestine and the rest of the civilized world, had established bell towers in town centers to regulate labor and commerce by ringing daily. The public bells would toll throughout the day, beginning approximately at 6:00 a.m. (at the first or Prime hour of the day). They rang again around 9:00 a.m. (the third hour, Terce), noon (sixth hour, Sext), 3:00 p.m. (the ninth hour, None), and at 6:00 p.m. to signal the end of the workday. The Gospels and the Acts of the Apostles indicate that certain key events took place at such times. The one who related the crucifixion of Jesus would have had no trouble in determining the hour of darkness nor the time of his death, for the Roman bell in Jerusalem would have tolled the noon and 3:00 hours, enabling the writer to determine that "it was about noon as darkness came over the whole land until three in the afternoon" (Luke 23:44), the hour that Jesus expired. Luke later told of Cornelius (Acts 10:1–9), who would have known that his angelic vision occurred about 3:00 in the afternoon because he would have heard the bell in Ceasarea toll the None hour. Following the angel's direction, Cornelius sent a delegation in search of Peter that arrived in Joppa around noon the next day. As they were approaching the city they would have heard the ringing of the midday bell, as would Peter, who "went up on the roof to pray." Peter hadn't gone to the roof to hide—he was following his daily custom of noontime prayer at Sext.

It seems almost charming to us today to note

that nearly all the New Testament references to time refer to these bell toll hours. We find no references to 9:45 a.m. or 3:15 p.m. In their best estimation, the writers determined that things happened around the third hour or the ninth hour of the day.

Up on the roof, we recall Peter praying the noontime prayers. He probably would have preferred to offer midday prayer in a local synagogue, but he was caught in an unfamiliar place. He prayed where he could find privacy. Jesus would have seen devout Jews praying in places other than the synagogue or temple as the city bells tolled. For this reason he chided the Pharisees in his Sermon on the Mount for praying at the street corners "so that they may be seen by others" (Matthew 6:5). Certainly the hyper-religious Pharisees would have planned their days to incorporate noonday prayer and would have known how much time was needed for travel to the synagogue. But, as Jesus observed, if they

carefully dawdled before noon, the time for prayer would catch them hurrying toward the synagogue or temple. Conspicuously stopping to pray at the street corner, then, would give to all observers the impression of scrupulous devotion. Jesus thought this was simply unscrupulous.

Those who made it successfully to the synagogue for worship would have heard many prayers, some scriptural readings, and the singing of psalms. The psalms would have been intoned as chant, either cantillated by a song leader (cantor) or sung responsively between cantor and congregation. Cantillation, in its simplest form, is the connection of vocalizations, stringing words together into melodic phrases. Some melodies were spontaneously made as the cantor shaped phrases according to the natural rise and fall in pitch of ordinary speech. Alternatively, a text would be chanted on a given tone, with perhaps, a single pitch modulation at the end of a phrase. Eventually, standardized melodies made their way into the psalm repertoire. The melodies of these psalm tones are long lost to history but would surely have had the tonality of early Semitic music. Yet, there is evidence that some of the oldest monastic chants retain traces of early Jewish psalm melodies. This can be explained, perhaps, by understanding that early Christians followed established Jewish practice in chanting the psalms and that the early centuries of Christian practice would have preserved what it received. Such is the nature of oral cultures.

Little is known about the state of singing in the private and public devotion of Christians in the first three centuries. Writers from the period indicate that believers sang as a regular practice, taking their texts from the psalms and the canticles. Canticles are biblical texts set to music. Perhaps the greatest example of these is Mary's song from Luke 1:46–56: "My soul magnifies the Lord...."

Beginnings of the Monastic Tradition and Prayer without End

Beginning in Egypt, and eventually spreading throughout the Christian world, there were individuals and groups of lay believers who became disinterested in the ecclesiastical structures of the city churches and began to set themselves apart. Anthony, born around 251 CE, is believed to be the originator of this movement. He practiced an extreme form of asceticism in which he removed himself to the Egyptian desert to live a life of prayer, fasting, celibacy, and contemplation. Others followed Anthony's example, becoming hermits who lived alone in caves or in the wilderness. Those who sought the contemplative life in community became monks or nuns and dwelled in buildings or villages called monasteries.

The cloistered life allowed the monastics to pray throughout the day. While exact historical information for this period is lacking, by the fourth century, it is clear that monks and nuns were praying, as did their Jewish forebears, at set hours of the day and night and that a central part of their prayer was the singing of psalms, canticles, and hymns. Their practice of singing and praying throughout the day and night established in a literal sense what Paul may have intended as figurative: "pray without ceasing" (1 Thessalonians 5:17). As the sun moved across the Middle East and North Africa, monastic communities prayed at the traditional times. Thus, the midday prayer of one community would be handed off to the noontime prayer of another community as the sun established local noon at every monastery on its journey westward. To this day, monastic communities hand off the prayer from time zone to time zone as communities gather for prayer day and night around the globe. To pray the Hours today is to join in the ceaseless prayer and endless song of the church through all generations.

The Rule of St. Benedict

Benedict of Nursia was born in 480 CE and died at the monastery he founded at Monte Cassino in 543. He is known as the father of the Western monastic tradition. What would he have heard and seen?

Benedict, the son of an Italian nobleman from the city of Nursia, was raised and educated in Rome. He would have heard the city bells tolling times for work and prayer. He would have seen a church that had the privilege of state support, yet one that was as corrupt in places as it was devout in others.

An unusually pious young man, Benedict recoiled from his secular education and the rampant sinfulness he saw about him. He fled from Rome as a young man to seek a life among "virtuous men," as his biographer, St. Gregory, put it. He became aware of those ascetic men who lived as hermits away from society in order to devote themselves to a life of continuous prayer.

For three years, Benedict sought distance from the evil he beheld in society by living in a cave as a hermit. He was ministered to and fed regularly by visits from a local monk named Romanus. Benedict's spirit and character matured during these years of separation. Even though he lived alone, his piety became known to local monasteries. When the abbot of a neighborhood monastery died, its brothers implored Benedict to serve as the leader of their community. Benedict had his doubts, fearing that his leadership would be too strict for the community. Nonetheless, he gave it a try. His doubts were confirmed when the monks tried to free themselves from his tight reign by poisoning his wine. According to legend, the cup shattered when Benedict made the sign of the cross over it while offering a blessing.

Benedict found greater receptivity for his ideas when he moved on to the city of Subiaco, where he established twelve small monasteries. These were not hermitic enclaves but communities of men who lived faithfully together, sharing common work, teaching local children, preaching to townspeople, devoting themselves to four hours of Bible reading and study per day, and attending regular hours of prayer where they recited Scripture and chanted the Psalter. From Subiaco, Benedict moved to establish the monastery for which he is best known, Monte Cassino. It was here that he wrote what is known as the Rule of St. Benedict.

Benedict's rule is a set of guidelines established to direct and govern the life of a monastic community. So thoughtfully did it organize communities for living according to gospel standards, it became the basic template for most other monastic communities and orders that followed. Within this rule, Benedict called for both private prayer by community members as well as public worship. In addition to daily Eucharist, the public prayers were to occur in intervals throughout the day, including a service deep in the night and

seven additional hours of prayer during the day. He scheduled these times of prayer to correspond to the ringing of city bells which tolled to signal the changing of the imperial guard in Rome. As the world focused on its secular rulers, Benedict wanted believers to pause in contemplation of the Divine ruler and the kingdom of heaven. Benedict's fixed hours of prayer included the singing of psalms and other devotional material as well as readings from Scripture and prayers. The psalms were to be cycled in such a way that the entire Psalter could be sung in a week. The fixed Hours of public worship came to be understood as the chief work of the monks and to be known as the *opus Dei*, the work of God. The common English form of this Latin term is the Divine Office. It represents a life of ceaseless prayer.

The power of this endless pattern of prayer can still be felt today, even by those who choose to visit the practice without making it a lifetime commitment. I recall vividly the first time I entered into a full twenty-four hour celebration of the Divine Office. Meeting as part of a Fuller Seminary course on Medieval Spirituality in a monastery in Orvieto, Italy, our community of faculty and students began with Vespers, just before dinner time. We prayed Compline (so named because it occurs at the completion of the day) around 9:00 p.m., and kept the night Vigils at midnight. We awakened at 3:00 a.m. to trundle down a dark hallway toward the chapel in slippers and bathrobes to celebrate

Lauds (meaning praise). Thirty minutes later I collapsed into bed in the Spartan monastery room to get a few more hours of sleep. As my head hit the hard pillow I recall thinking with a mixture of surprised joy and fatigue, "It seems like all I do is pray anymore!" If a Protestant visitor to the Hours can be so overwhelmed with a sense of endless prayer, it is surely true that those who give themselves to such devotion daily and throughout their lives must bask in the knowledge of God's presence and power in all they do.

One of the lasting results of Benedict's rule was the introduction of the *Gloria Patri* to the office of daily prayers. This is an ancient Trinitarian blessing affixed to the psalms as a means by which to baptize them for Christian use. The Latin name means "Glory to the Father," and it concludes with the now familiar "and to the Son, and to the Holy Spirit. As it was in the beginning, is now and ever shall be, world without end, Amen."

Another of the lasting results of Benedict's rule was the regulation of the times for fixed-hour prayer. He called for daily prayers to occur eight times during the day. This created an octave of prayer that corresponds to the eight tones in a musical octave. The practice of ceaseless prayer is intrinsically wedded to the patterns of endless song. These fixed-hour times of prayer have become the standard pattern for cloistered life, whether the order is Benedictine, Dominican, Franciscan, or another. In some communities today, the eight times of prayer are reduced to six or fewer, thus limiting the interruptions of sleep and work. Nonetheless, strict adherence to pausing during the day and rising during the night to praise God is the norm for praying the Divine Office. While there are variations in the way that the Hours are named and scheduled, there is a pattern that is most commonly followed:

VESPERS. As in Jewish practice, the monastic day begins at sundown. From the Latin for evening, Vespers is prayed as the new day begins. Its traditional focus is on Christ as the Light of the world.

COMPLINE is prayed before bedtime. The simple life of monastic communities makes it possible for its members to retire around 9:00 p.m. The purpose of Compline is both to prepare one for sleep and to reflect on our final sleep in death.

VIGILS is the night office, requiring people to rise from sleep at midnight. Some may find it convenient to remain awake until the vigil has been kept. This is the time for earnest wakefulness, where we learn to trust God in the darkness.

LAUDS is the early morning time of praise. It may fall anywhere from 3:00 a.m. to just before sunrise. It is a time of prayer for the coming of the sun and with it the possibilities of the dawning day. Matins (from the Latin word for morning) is a term sometimes associated with this time of day and is often used as a synonym for Lauds. In some practices, Matins is a separate time of prayer that precedes Lauds.

PRIME is prayed at the beginning of the workday, about 6:00 or 7:00 a.m. The worker is fully awake, ready to set his or her sights on the tasks ahead. Traditionally, Prime is a meditation on Creation. It also reflects upon the appearance of Jesus before Caiaphas in the Passion narrative, an event that took place before dawn (Matthew 26:57–68).

TERCE, the third hour. The workday is well underway. Yet the worker pauses to remember that there is a purpose greater than the task at hand; it is an awareness of God. The traditional meditation of Terce is on the Holy Spirit, who appeared at this hour on the day of Pentecost (Acts 2:1–15).

SEXT, midday, the sixth hour of the workday. The success of the day's work hangs in balance. The pause to pray reflects upon the awareness that half of the day is spent. It is a metaphor for midlife, when we remember our youthful exuberance and we pray for remaining strength. Because this was the time of day during which Jesus hung upon the cross (Mark 15:33), Sext is a time to reflect upon his anguish, even as we meditate upon the crosses with which we are burdened.

NONE occurs at mid-afternoon. The workday is nearly spent, as is the energy of the worker. Even so was the vigor of Christ, who died at this hour (Mark 15:34–38).

The marriage of chant to fixed hours of prayer occurred long before Benedict. His communities simply carried on the traditions of singing the psalms, hymns, and canticles that they received. The music was simple, merely a melody line that would sound austere to modern ears. As chant developed, it became more complex and harmonious. Yet what we hear today as monastic chant derives from this strong tradition of singing a text in unison on a few musical tones in order that the text be articulated with clarity and prayerfulness. Chant, in one form or another, is a common practice in all of the world's great religions. Those accustomed to chant, whether through singing or listening, become aware of its power to absorb human consciousness, deepen the experience of meditation, and create an awareness of holiness and wholeness. Studies have even shown that chanting can have a healing effect on those who practice it over a long period of time. For these reasons, chant has endured throughout the Middle Ages and into our time as a means of expressing that which is too deep for words. Because faith resides at the soul-deep level of human experience, people require tools to plumb such sentient depths. Art serves this function, and the simple form of art known as chant evokes a resonance between singer and listener, between one person praying and another, even between ourselves and God.

When we do not know how to pray as we ought, we can accept chant as a musical form of the Spirit-borne sigh that intercedes for us as Paul promised in Romans 8:26.

There is another reason for the enduring character of chant; it can be found in the great stone cathedrals of Europe. Due to the acoustic properties of buildings made of massive masonry, the sound of the spoken word is masked by layers of echo that bounce from near and far along the interiors, arches, and angles of large churches. The speaking voice, with its inflections and variances in volume, creates harmonic patterns that, when echoed and amplified, become overwhelming in such an acoustically wet environment. Chant, on the other hand, reduces the range, volume, and inflectional variables in the voice. The corresponding harmonics and echoes are reduced to such an extent that when chanted, words can be heard with greater clarity. It is possible to test this acoustic property when visiting such churches. A speaker need only talk in a normal tone of voice at a distance of, say, fifty feet and ask if the listeners can understand the words. Then, the same words can be chanted on a single tone. Listeners will invariably announce that the words are more audible when they are chanted.

Gregorian Chant and Its Kin

Pope Gregory the Great (540–604 CE) is credited with the compilation of the chants used in the Divine Office and in the Roman Catholic Mass. This is the same Gregory that recorded sketches on St. Benedict's life in his *Dialogues*. There are legends that say that Gregory composed many of the chants by merely writing down what an angel sang into his ear. Most likely, he did not compose Gregorian chants, but they came to be known by his name because under his guidance, scattered chants were compiled into a single collection that was copied and made available to the churches under his papal care. Gregorian chant

was not the only type of chant available in Middle Age Europe. There were other chant dialects, such as Celtic, Gallican, Ambrosian, and Mozarabic. Under the Holy Roman Empire reign of Charlemagne (800–814 CE) and with his encouragement, these chant dialects were suppressed while Gregorian chant was imposed, along with the use of Latin as the standard language for worship, throughout the empire.

Gregorian chant is also known as plain chant or plain song. This term distinguishes simple, monophonic (single part) chant from the polyphonic chant (many parts sung simultaneously) that developed between the ninth and twelfth centuries.

Plain chant was the norm in the church in the West for centuries, but interest in it and practice of it began to wane in the fourteenth century as polyphony became more popular for use in Eucharistic worship. Its use and forms deteriorated so much that by the nineteenth century, plain chant was rarely used. Still, the practice was not lost to the church. In 1860, a French Benedictine monastery in Solemses undertook the task of restoring the archives and the practice of Gregorian chant. Its monks worked for decades compiling the ancient chants and restoring them to their thirteenth-century forms. It is this type of chant that can be found on modern-day recordings, most notably the 1994 recording of *Chant*, made by the Benedictine monks of the monastery at Santo Domingo de Silos in Spain. This album has sold over two million copies, inspiring *Time* magazine to report that "Gregorian Chant has suddenly become America's newest pop-music phenomenon."

Today, another form of chant has become popular in the church in the West. A cousin of plain chant, this dialect is best described as cyclical chant. It was made popular through the music of the Taizé community in France. This ecumenical group of brothers has established a place of retreat for young Christians traveling in Europe. Their community grew out of the work of their founder, Brother Roger, who struggled during World War II to help Jewish and other refugees fleeing from the Nazis. Following the war, the growing community even gave aid to German ex-prisoners of war.

The song of this community was developed in a simple chant form that takes for its text lines from prayers, Scripture (such as "Jesus, remember me when you come into your kingdom," Luke 23:42), and classic religious declarations (*"Ubi caritas, et amor; ubi caritas, Deus ibi est,"* or "Where there is charity and love, there is God"). The song texts are often in Latin, not because they intend to be reminiscent of Roman Catholic chants, but because Latin is highly singable and because it doesn't privilege any of the native languages spoken by the young people who flock to Taizé from around the world. The chants are sometimes sung in various languages and occasionally in several languages at once. The intention for these cyclical chants is to sing them repeatedly, as often as desired. Each might be sung between two and ten times, perhaps even more. Their melodies are short and simple and allow for spontaneous harmonization. The repetition of the chants allows for two things to happen. Repeating the chants can draw the singer and the community deeply into contemplation where text and music balance between mystery and awareness, hewing channels of resonance through which deep calls to deep. The repetition also allows for the chants to assume the musical form of theme and variations. Some of the musical variety is achieved as voices invent harmonies. More variety is added when flutes or other instruments perform *obbligato* melodies composed to add depth to the musical arrangements.

Cyclical chants are dissimilar to Gregorian chant in that they are typically arranged for part-singing and incorporate various forms of simple instrumental accompaniment. Yet, what they have in common with plain chant is the ability to bring modern-day worshipers into a numinous space as prayers are borne upon currents of song. Like waves upon a beach, the song-prayer recycles, each wave turning over new stones of awareness and depositing treasures from unplumbable depths.

Some of the chants found in the orders for the Divine Office contained in this book follow traditional patterns for singing the psalms and canticles. Their use is described in the chapter, "How to Use This Book." The refrains prepared for each of the eight Hours in this book are of the cyclical chant form. Their purpose is to draw worshipers into participation in the ancient practice of ceaseless prayer and endless song.

—*Clay Schmit*

THE HOURS

† group designation for antiphonal singing or reading

‡ alternate group designation for antiphonal singing or reading

Ω indicates portions of the liturgy where worshipers may kneel

vespers

VESPERS

Sundown. We gather together.

The sun recedes, we worship You.
We eat, we pray, we drink, we sing.
Hinei mah tov umah na'im
(Behold, how good and how pleasant it is)
shevet achim gam yachad.
(for brethren to dwell together in unity.)

VESPERS REFRAIN

There is a reason why the light at Vespers is referred to by filmmakers as "magic hour." It is the end of the day. The light is golden, throwing shadows that are pleasing at this comfortable time, shadows that will become suspicious and

threatening as the night deepens. It is an hour weary but beautiful with a life well-lived, an hour of fellowship, when people gather to share food and each other's company. Vespers is a bookend to Lauds, the other hinge hour of the day, completing the sun's slow arc through the sky. We see each other differently in its golden light, as if newly met; we see ourselves differently as reflected in the eyes of those who love us, and we believe that we have done well. Together we are able to keep the challenge of Vespers—to let go of the disappointments of the day, and to embrace life as we embrace one another: with

sincere, full-bodied joy.

Night comes, accompanied by a visible sundown or not. Even if obscured by weather, the dark still comes, slowly and almost imperceptibly, as when the heart realizes that the hoped-for will not come. What of when the wind and the rain are strong enough to shudder candle flames on the table inside, and the setting sun of Vespers is invisible? When sorrow likewise prevails, and hope slips beneath the horizon under cover of a cloudy sky—can we celebrate Vespers then? Fuller Theological Seminary Professor David Scholer gave the 2008 baccalaureate speech shortly before he died.[14] He sat behind a great table on the sanctuary stage, and it was as though he had invited us to join him at dinner. Though too weak in body to stand, he was not weak in voice, and he delivered the speech of our lives, urging us to love. His sundown happened too soon, even though his life was full of purpose until the end. He reminded us that life is not about us, but about God. And we believed him.

Polish playwright Vaclav Havel wrote, "Whether all is really lost or not depends entirely on whether or not I am lost."[15] At Vespers, we lay aside petty grievances and forgive, we eat together and we bless. When we gather we find a new energy because we receive it from one another. This is how one keeps from getting lost. It is a time when Jesus himself joins us, to confirm our faith and to allay our fears: "Truly I tell you, whatever you bind on earth will be bound in heaven, and whatever you loose on earth will be loosed in heaven. Again, truly I tell you, if two of you agree on earth about anything you ask, it will be done for you by my Father in heaven. For where two or three are gathered in my name, I am there among them" (Mt 18:18–21).

At Vespers, we light candles to say, "I know the sun has set, but I light a new light against the darkness as a reminder that the sun will rise again." This is Vespers rest—the finish of one day and hope of another, and the faith of mysteries between. With Mary, we pray the Magnificat: "My soul magnifies the Lord, and my spirit rejoices in God my Savior, for He has looked with favor on the lowliness of His servant. Surely, from now on all generations will call me blessed; for the Mighty One has done great things for me, and holy is His name. His mercy is for those who fear Him from generation to generation. He has shown strength with His arm; He has scattered the proud in the thoughts of their hearts. He has brought down the powerful from their thrones, and lifted up the lowly; He has filled the hungry with good things, and sent the rich away empty." (Luke 1:46–53).

Ich habe Hymnen, die ich schweige

I have hymns that I have not sung.
I am out of your reach, but my heart bows toward you:
You think of me as great, but I am near.

You can hardly distinguish me
from those who kneel;
they are like grazing flocks,
and I am the watching shepherd on the hillside.

In the dusk they return home, and I follow them.
I listen to their thudding on dark bridges,
and the rising mist from their backs
veils my return.

RAINER MARIA RILKE, *The Book of Hours,* I, 40

VESPERS LITURGY

THE INVOCATION

> **All:** Your word is a lamp to my feet and a light to my path. Accept my offerings of praise,
> O Lord, and teach me your ordinances.

(Psalm 119: 105, 108)

THE GREETING

> **All:** The grace of our Lord Jesus Christ, the love of God, and the communion of the Holy Spirit
> be with us. Amen.

(2 Corinthians 13:13)

THE VESPERS REFRAIN

The sun re cedes, we wor ship You. We eat, we pray, we drink, we sing.

Hi - nei mah tove u - mah na' - im she - vet a - chim gam ya - chad.

PSALM 18 *(sung in unison)*

I love you, O　　　　/ Lord.　*　O Lord　　　\ my　　　　　/ strength.

The Lord is my rock, my fortress, and my deliverer, my God,
　　　　　my rock in whom I take /refuge,
　　*my shield, and the horn of my salvation, \my /stronghold.

 I call upon the Lord, who is worthy to be /praised,
　　*so I shall be saved from \my /enemies.

For I have kept the ways of the /Lord,
　　*and have not wickedly departed from \my /God.

For all his ordinances were be/fore me,
　　*and his statutes I did not put a\way from /me.

I was blameless be/fore him,
　　*and I kept myself \from /guilt.

Therefore the Lord has recompensed me according to my /righteousness,
　　*according to the cleanness of my hands in \his /sight.

For you deliver a humble /people,
　　*but the haughty eyes you \bring /down.

It is you who light my /lamp;
    *the Lord, my God, lights up \my /darkness.

This God—his way is perfect; the promise of the Lord proves /true;
    *he is a shield for all who take refuge \in /him.

For who is God except the / Lord?
    *And who is a rock besides \our /God?—

the God who girded me with /strength,
    *and made my \way /safe.

He made my feet like the feet of a /deer,
    *and set me secure \on the /heights.

For this I will extol you, O Lord, among the /nations,
    *and sing praises \to your /name.

Great triumphs he gives to his/ king,
    *and shows steadfast love to his anointed, to David and
        his \descendents for /ever.

GLORIA PATRI *(sung in like manner)*

Glory be to the Father and the Son and the Holy /Spirit.
    *As it was in the beginning, is now and ever shall be. \A/men.

THE VESPERS REFRAIN *(see above)*

READING

The Magnificat, Luke 1:39–55 *(read antiphonally)*

† In those days Mary set out and went with haste to a Judean town in the hill country, where she entered the house of Zechariah and greeted Elizabeth. When Elizabeth heard Mary's greeting, the child leaped in her womb. And Elizabeth was filled with the Holy Spirit and exclaimed with a loud cry, "Blessed are you among women, and blessed is the fruit of your womb. And why has this happened to me, that the mother of my Lord comes to me? For as soon as I heard the sound of your greeting, the child in my womb leaped for joy. And blessed is she who believed that there would be a fulfillment of what was spoken to her by the Lord."

‡ And Mary said, "My soul magnifies the Lord, and my spirit rejoices in God my Savior, for he has looked with favor on the lowliness of his servant. Surely, from now on all generations will call me blessed; for the Mighty One has done great things for me, and holy is his name. His mercy is for those who fear him from generation to generation. He has shown strength with his arm; he has scattered the proud in the thoughts of their hearts. He has brought down the powerful from their thrones, and lifted up the lowly; he has filled the hungry with good things, and sent the rich away empty. He has helped his servant Israel, in remembrance of his mercy, according to the promise he made to our ancestors, to Abraham and to his descendants forever."

THE VESPERS REFRAIN *(see above)*

SILENCE Ω

HYMN: PHOS HILARON *(Greek hymn)*

O Gladsome Light of the holy glory of the Immortal / Father,

* heavenly, holy, blessed Je \ sus / Christ.

Now we have come to the setting of the /sun
       *and behold the light \of /evening.

We praise /God:
       *Father, Son, and Ho\ly /Spirit.

For it is right at all times to worship You with voices of /praise,
       *O Son of God and Giver \of /Life.

Therefore all the /world
       *glori\fies /You.

O Gladsome Light of the holy glory of the Immortal /Father,
       *heavenly, holy, blessed Je\sus /Christ.

THE LORD'S PRAYER Ω

THE PRAYERS Ω

THE VESPERS REFRAIN *(see above)*

THE SENDING
> **One:** Let us go in peace, guided by the light of Christ in all we do.
> **All:** Amen.

In the strictest tradition, monastic communities gather for prayer eight times a day, every day. Within a week, they pray through the entire Psalter. The list below provides Psalm suggestions for Vespers, for use by communities desiring to use these liturgies in praying the Divine Office upon successive days:

Psalms 109, 110, 111, 112, 113, 114, 115, 119, 120, 121, 122, 123, 124, 125, 126, 127, 128, 129, 130, 131, 132, 135, 136, 137, 138, 139, 140, 141, 142, 143, 144

compline

COMPLINE

The moon has risen. We enter the night rest.

You lay me down
in the arms of night,
You guard and teach me
as I dream.

COMPLINE REFRAIN

Each night, when the moon has conquered the horizon of day and the sky has dimmed, we anticipate the release into sleep. With or against our wills, sleep will overtake us, even if we fight with all our strength, as most children do.

Enforced sleeplessness is, in fact, a form of torture, for we are designed to cycle between wakefulness and dreams, much as the earth keeps its similar and accommodating rhythms. It is an inviolable cycle of nature.

Like so many wonders of our lives, sleep is made common by its familiarity. But think of it— we rehearse this little death with hardly a thought of the bizarre and unknown world we enter. We are lulled there by our own weariness, by some internal knowledge, and yet what state could be more strange, more intimidating? In the night, when "like a roaring lion your adversary the devil prowls around, looking for someone to devour," we are dragged through the portal of sleep into dreams, into a world hidden from consciousness. Vulnerable, without the awareness allowed even to Alice, we spend nearly half our lives in a wonderland of absurdity. Into that dark we go alone, as if in a fairy tale or horror film, only to emerge with little memory of where we have been or for how long.

God has shaped us so that we are forced to keep this Sabbath of the body, and yet he has left keeping the Sabbath of the soul to our inadequate discretion. Why so insistent and inscrutable a strategy? The Psalmist urges for a balance not often considered: "It is vain for you to rise up early, To retire late, To eat the bread of painful labors; For He gives to His beloved even in his sleep" (Psalm 127:2 NAS).

What happens to our spirits as we sleep? The author of the hymn best known for its last verse, the "doxology," Thomas Ken wrote in another verse, "when in the night I sleepless be, my soul with heavenly thoughts supply."[16] Ken implies that dreams might be vessels for a form of God's wisdom that is above or beyond conscious thought. The suffering servant Job agrees, "In a dream, for instance," he recounts, "a vision at night, when men and women are deep in sleep, fast asleep in their beds—God opens their ears and impresses them with warnings to turn them back from something bad they're planning, from some reckless choice, and keep them from an early grave, from the river of no return" (33:15–18, *The Message*).

Here is a mystery then: why not enter sleep as though embarking on a great journey into the unknown—a journey for which we might actually prepare? Why not go into sleep with intention and prayers for guidance? In this hour of Compline, we are urged by the ancients to request nourishing and learning dreams from the One who never sleeps, who never slumbers. So perhaps we may request the presence of God not just "my soul to keep" but to accompany us, like Virgil with Dante, into the hells and heavens played out in our sleeping hours, and to teach us these life-preserving things that would remain otherwise hidden.

"A peaceful night and a perfect end give us," the monks pray in this hour. The Compline hymn requests defense through the night against danger and terror, protection against evil. Yet Compline is a contemplative office characterized by spiritual peace. In many monasteries it is the custom to begin the "Great Silence" after Compline, during which the whole community, including guests, observe silence throughout the night until the morning service the next day. "Be vigilant!" those entering this great silence are warned, "you are entering the night rest." Yes, be vigilant and keep silence, but do so in order to listen. Learn from the hour of Compline not to fear death but to anticipate its wonder, for to succumb at the end of each of each day is the same as with the sum of them—to journey toward morning.

Ich lebe mein Leben in wachsenden Ringen

I live my life in ever-increasing circles
that stretch across all things.
I may not manage to complete the final circle
still I must attempt it.

I revolve around God, the tower of old,
and I spin amidst thousands of years.
Yet I remain unclear of my role—
am I a falcon,
a storm,
or a beautiful song?

RAINER MARIA RILKE, *The Book of Hours,* I, 2

COMPLINE LITURGY

THE INVOCATION

All: To you, O Lord, I call; my rock, do not refuse to hear me. Hear the voice of my supplication, as I cry to you for help, as I lift up my hands toward your most holy sanctuary.

(Psalm 28: 1, 2)

THE GREETING

One: The Lord be with you.

All: And also with you.

One: Lift up your hearts.

All: We lift them up to the Lord our God.

One: Let us give thanks to the Lord our God.

All: It is right that we give Him thanks and praise.

THE COMPLINE REFRAIN

You lay me down in the arms of night. You guard me and teach me

as I dream. Guard me and teach me as I dream.

PSALM 34 *(sung antiphonally on a single tone)*

† I will bless the Lord at all times; His praise shall continually be in my mouth.

‡ My soul makes its boast in the Lord; let the humble hear and be glad.

† O magnify the Lord with me, and let us exalt His name together.

‡ I sought the Lord, and He answered me, and delivered me from all my fears.

† Look to Him, and be radiant; so your faces shall never be ashamed.

‡ This poor soul cried, and was heard by the Lord, and was saved from every trouble.

† The angel of the Lord encamps around those who fear Him, and delivers them.

‡ O taste and see that the Lord is good; happy are those who take refuge in Him.

† O fear the Lord, you His holy ones, for those who fear Him have no want.

‡ The young lions suffer want and hunger, but those who seek the Lord lack no good thing.

† Come, O children, listen to me; I will teach you the fear of the Lord.

‡ Which of you desires life, and covets many days to enjoy good?

† Keep your tongue from evil, and your lips from speaking deceit.

‡ Depart from evil, and do good; seek peace, and pursue it.

† The eyes of the Lord are on the righteous, and His ears are open to their cry.

‡ The face of the Lord is against evildoers, to cut off the remembrance of them from the earth.

† When the righteous cry for help, the Lord hears, and rescues them from all their troubles.

‡ The Lord is near to the brokenhearted, and saves the crushed in spirit.

† Many are the afflictions of the righteous, but the Lord rescues them from them all.

‡ He keeps all their bones; not one of them will be broken.

† Evil brings death to the wicked, and those who hate the righteous will be condemned.

‡ The Lord redeems the life of His servants; none of those who take refuge in Him will be condemned.

GLORIA PATRI *(sung in like manner)*

† Glory to the Father and to the Son and to the Holy Spirit.

‡ As it was in the beginning, is now and ever shall be. Amen.

THE COMPLINE REFRAIN *(see above)*

READINGS

You, O Lord, are in the midst of us, and we are called by your name; do not forsake us!

(Jeremiah 14:9)

Do not worry, saying, "What will we eat?" or "What will we drink?" or "What will we wear?"… indeed your heavenly Father knows that you need all these things. But strive first for the kingdom of God and His righteousness, and all these things will be given to you as well. So do not worry about tomorrow.

(Matthew 6:31–34)

Come to me, all you that are weary and are carrying heavy burdens, and I will give you rest. Take my yoke upon you, and learn from me; for I am gentle and humble in heart, and you will find rest for your souls. For my yoke is easy and my burden is light.

(Matthew 11:28–30)

It is the God who said, "Let light shine out of darkness," who has shone in our hearts to give the light of the knowledge of the glory of God in the face of Jesus Christ. But we have this treasure in clay jars, so that it may be made clear that this extraordinary power belongs to God and does not come from us.

(2 Corinthians 4:6–7)

THE COMPLINE REFRAIN *(see above)*

HYMN: ALL PRAISE TO THEE, MY GOD THIS NIGHT

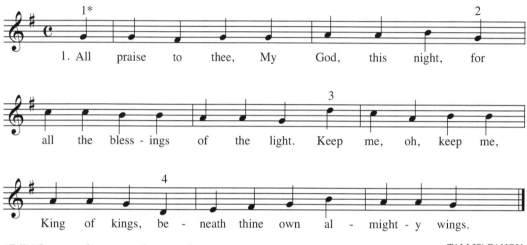

Tallis' Canon may be sung as a 4 part round.

TALLIS' CANON
Thomas Tallis, 1505-1585

2. Forgive me, Lord, for thy dear Son, the ill that I this day have done;
   That with the world, myself, and thee, I, ere I sleep, at peace may be.

3. Teach me to live, that I may dread the grave as little as my bed.
   Teach me to die, so that I may rise glorious at the awesome day.

4. Oh, may my soul in thee repose, and with sweet sleep my eyelids close,
   Sleep that shall me more vigorous make to serve my God when I awake.

5. Praise God from whom all blessings flow; Praise Him, all creatures here below;
Praise Him above, ye heavenly host; Praise Father, Son, and Holy Ghost.

(Thomas Ken, 1637–1711)

THE LORD'S PRAYER Ω

THE PRAYERS Ω *(prayers of confession are traditionally included at Compline)*

THE COMPLINE REFRAIN *(see above)*

THE SENDING

One: Let us bless the Lord.
All: Thanks be to God.
One: Almighty and merciful God, Father, Son, and Holy Spirit, bless, preserve, and keep us,
this night and forevermore.
All: Amen.

In the strictest tradition, monastic communities gather for prayer eight times a day, every day. Within a week, they pray through the entire Psalter. The list below provides Psalm suggestions for Compline, for use by communities desiring to use these liturgies in praying the Divine Office upon successive days:

Psalms 4, 6, 7, 11, 12, 15, 33, 60, 69, 70, 76, 85, 87, 90, 102, 129, 130, 131, 132, 133,
134, 135, 136, 137, 138, 139, 140, 148, 149, 150

vigils

VIGILS

The moon is overhead. The watchman waits.

Here I am,

here I am.

Your Servant, I AM.

VIGILS REFRAIN

Vigils is the night hour, the longest hour, the polar opposite of Sext at noon. Like the noon hour, the light source is overhead: but at midnight, the moon casts strange and sharp shadows that give the illusion of life to inanimate but familiar objects, redrawn by the darkness into threatening figures. Things happen at this hour that do not happen at any other time, lost souls wander, harm is plotted. The Vigils hours bridge the gap between sleep and sunrise, a dark purgatory where evildoer and intercessor alike find purpose. In the worship of false lords, the 3 a.m. hour is called the witching hour, a mockery of the time at three p.m. when Christ died. Vigils contains the drama of both righteousness and evil.

The Latin root of the word *vigil* means "wakefulness." To keep Vigils does not mean simply to be unable to rest, to be anxious or beleaguered by mind-revving sleeplessness. Keeping Vigils is rather to be purposefully awake at a time when one would otherwise (or surely rather) sleep. This element of intention to wakefulness is why "vigil" is also applied to some traditional devotional observances. In Eastern Orthodox and Roman Catholic traditions—as well as in many cultures—a vigil is sometimes held during the dark night when someone is gravely ill or dying, and can extend through to burial. In some ancient and often primitive cultures, this ritual had the practical application of protecting the body of a loved one from harm until buried "safely"—deep enough to be beyond violation by enemy, spirit, or animal.

Vigils is a time for prayers that are solitary, languid with the luxury of extended hours, and yet still on the *qui vive* required of a sentinel. The beautiful but heartbreaking description of sorrow found in Lamentations 3 is Jeremiah's consummate Vigils prayer, ending with: "My soul continually thinks of it and is bowed down within me. But this I call to mind, and therefore I have hope: The steadfast love of the Lord never ceases, his mercies never come to an end; they are new every morning; great is your faithfulness. 'The Lord is my portion,' says my soul, 'therefore I will hope in him'" (3:20–24).

The night watch is a boundaried wakefulness; to kill or waste time is to fail the watch and to ignore the nature of the *kairos* time in which it takes place. To remain awake and prayerful at Vigils, then, is a practiced discipline, but like the prophet Jeremiah's deep-night reflections, it is often an hour of melancholy and yearning for dawn: "my soul waits for the Lord more than those who watch for the morning, more than those who watch for the morning" (Psalm 130:6). The watchman, one is tempted to imagine, is thoughtful, grim, and made otherworldly himself by his duties.

The dark and the light are the same to God, the psalmist tells us. Silence is the soundtrack of this Hour, whispers and listening, mystery, danger, trust. The purpose of this time is to learn to trust God in the darkness. On the façade of the National Cathedral in Washington D.C. there is a statue of the archangel Michael keeping the night vigil. When the sun rises, it finds him with his sword finally lowered, because his watch is over at first light. Above the archangel is a gargoyle covering his ears and screaming at the sound of the trumpet blast of Lauds.

Ich bete wieder, du Erlauchter

Once again, I pray, your Majesty.
Once again, you hear me talk in the wind.
From my innermost being never-used words
gush forth in a mighty way.

I was confused:
my ego fractured, every piece of me was turned over to the enemy.
Oh God, the scornful scorned me, and drunks reveled in my misery.

I crept into people's back yards,
ate out of garbage cans and collected broken glass.
With my half-opened mouth I stammered
at You, who are full of grace.

I raised my tired hands to You, in nameless pleading,
that I would find my eyes again, with which I once beheld You.

I was a house, ruined by fire, where only murderers seek to rest
'til relentless law dogs them to a further place.

I was like a city, built by the sea, afflicted by a plague
that clings heavily, like a corpse, to the hands of children.

I was a stranger to myself.
Her broken heart pulsated her pain to me, in her womb.

But now, I am restored, assembled from pieces of my shameful past.
I yearn for Your holy covenant, for Your all-consuming wisdom
to preside over me.
I yearn for the magnificent hands of Your generous heart.
Oh, come closer.
Here is what counts—only my God and me,
and You have the right to squander me.

RAINER MARIA RILKE, *The Book of Hours,* II, 2

VIGILS LITURGY

THE INVOCATION

All: Hear my cry, O God; listen to my prayer. From the end of the earth I call to you, when my heart is faint. Lead me to the rock that is higher than I; for you are my refuge, a strong tower against the enemy.

(Psalm 61:1–3)

THE GREETING

All: Almighty God grant us a quiet night and peace at the last. Amen.

THE VIGILS REFRAIN

Here I am, here I am, your ser-vant, I am.

Here I am, here I am, your ser-vant, I AM.

PSALM 16 *(sung in unison)*

Protect me, O God,   for in you I \ take / refuge.

I say to the Lord, "You are my Lord; I have no good a\part from /you."

As for the holy ones in the land, they are the noble, in \whom is all my de/light.

The Lord is my chosen portion and my cup; you \hold my /lot.

The boundary lines have fallen for me in pleasant places; I have a \goodly /heritage.

I bless the Lord who gives me counsel; in the night also my \heart instructs /me.

I keep the Lord always before me; because He is at my right hand, I shall \not be /moved.

Therefore my heart is glad, and my soul rejoices; my body also \rests se/cure.

For You do not give me up to Sheol, or let Your faithful one \see the /Pit.

You show me the \path of /life.

In Your presence there is fullness of joy; in Your right hand are \pleasures forever/more.

GLORIA PATRI *(sung in like manner)*

Glory to the Father and to the Son and to the \Holy /Spirit.

As it was in the beginning, is now and ever shall be. \A/men.

THE VIGILS REFRAIN *(see above)*

READINGS

> The sun shall no longer be your light by day, nor for brightness shall the moon give light to you by night; but the Lord will be your everlasting light, and your God will be your glory.
>
> (Isaiah 60:19)

> I am convinced that neither death, nor life, nor angels, nor rulers, nor things present, nor things to come, nor powers, nor height, nor depth, nor anything else in all creation, will be able to separate us from the love of God in Christ Jesus our Lord.
>
> (Romans 8:38–39)

> When this perishable body puts on imperishability, and this mortal body puts on immortality, then the saying will be fulfilled: "Death has been swallowed up in victory." "Where, O death, is your victory? Where, O death, is your sting?"
>
> (1 Corinthians 15:54–55)

THE VIGILS REFRAIN *(see above)*

SILENCE Ω

HYMN: NOW THE DAY IS OVER

1. Now the day is ov - er; night is draw-ing nigh. ___

Shad - ows of the eve - ning steal a-cross the sky.

MERRIAL
Joseph Barnaby, 1838-1896

2. Jesus give the weary calm and sweet repose;
   With Your tenderest blessing, may our eyelids close.

3. Comfort every sufferer watching late in pain.
   Those who plan some evil, from their sin restrain.

4. Through the long night-watches may your angels spread
   Their bright wings above me, watching round my bed.

5. When the morning wakens, then may I arise
   Pure and fresh and sinless in Your holy eyes.

6. Glory to the Father, glory to the Son,
   And to You blest Spirit, while the ages run.

(Sabine Baring-Gould, 1834–1924)

THE LORD'S PRAYER Ω

THE PRAYERS Ω

THE VIGILS REFRAIN *(see above)*

THE CLOSING PRAYER

> **All:** Watch now, dear Lord, with those who watch or weep tonight, and give Your angels charge over those who sleep. Tend Your sick ones, Lord Christ, rest Your weary ones, bless Your dying ones, soothe Your suffering ones, pity Your afflicted ones, shield Your joyous ones, and all for Your love's sake. And may the God of hope fill us with all joy and peace in believing, that we may abound in hope by the power of the Holy Spirit. Amen.
>
> (based on Psalms 3–5; 121; 130; Romans 15:13)

In the strictest tradition, monastic communities gather for prayer eight times a day, every day. Within a week, they pray through the entire Psalter. The list below provides Psalm suggestions for Vigils, for use by communities desiring to use these liturgies in praying the Divine Office upon successive days:

Psalms 1, 2, 3, 8, 9, 10, 13, 14, 16, 17, 19, 20, 29, 34, 36, 37, 38, 44, 45, 47, 48, 49, 50, 61, 65, 67, 68, 77, 78, 80, 82, 94, 104, 105, 106, 118

LAUDS

The sun returns. The sleeper awakes.

I am in all things naked.

Spirit, clothe me in the light.

LAUDS REFRAIN

This Hour is one of two most easily identified by the movement of celestial light. Sunrise and sunset—Lauds and Vespers—are called hinge Hours, because they are transitions between dark and light. Their separation defined the world's first and therefore iconic drama. The Hour of Lauds marks the time from the sky's first lightening to the sun's release into the sky from the horizon. The light changes quickly, radically, to throw a pale, clean, hopeful hue on the world. Joy replaces mourning at this hour, according to the Scriptures.

The personality of Lauds is to be found in all things naked and new. It is a time of relief, of celebration, liveliness, and, as Paul urges the Corinthians in his first letter to them, an hour to follow after love. "The Morning Office" is one of the most ancient offices and can be traced back to apostolic times in the sixth century.

Not all dawns bring joy, however, and those who suffer in the night hours are often wary of dawn. They bury their heads under the false night of a pillow or blanket, not simply tired but exhausted by vigils well over one night long, and full of pain. What kind of Lauds awaits King David, after a sleepless night: "I rise before dawn and cry for help; I put my hope in your words. My eyes are awake before each watch of the night, that I may meditate on your promise" (Psalm 119:147–48).

As with each Hour, the citizen of Lauds faces the sometimes brutal conflict between dreams and reality, voicing the ubiquitous surprise that "things didn't turn out the way I expected them to." What does it cost to face the challenge of Lauds for the woman who dreams of family and wakes alone? Will she choose love when she can no longer imagine its shape? To be found naked at Lauds may mean revealing a life like a hard crust of bread rather than the scent of orange blossoms. So this hour is also a soul-hinge, shifting from darkness into light when often only the darkness can be imagined.

Spanish poet Juan Ramón Jiménez wrote the simple lines: "My boat struck something deep. And nothing changed, and everything has changed. And here I sit in the middle of my new life." This is a Lauds prayer. What is, *is*. What is not, is *not*. New and not new, this sleepy, achy hour is where God meets us with tender urgings toward courage. We must be led into the light by the Spirit who knows and sees things hidden to us, for sorrow is always easier to anticipate than

joy. Joy is the Spirit's surprise, delivered through the humblest of messengers, impossible to imagine or control. How can a season of heartache be relieved—even temporarily—by the random sight of a hummingbird? The sound of a child's singing voice? A genuine soul-laugh or a scent that excavates a deeply treasured memory?

It is impossible to plan on a breeze lightening relentless sorrow or depression, and yet it happens. God must glory in these astonishing victories of the poignant over the crushing, because it is a device unique to his service. A holocaust survivor tells of concentration camp misery being relieved by the song of a morning bird. A mother keeping watch at the children's hospital is given hope by the smile of a sick child. Rage is turned aside by a soft word. Such tender mercies are potent because they are reminders of God's presence in our days, His intimacy. The Lover of our Souls is the man of our dreams, the soulmate, the beloved brother, father, and comforter. He watches over us in the night, as He promises, He guides us through dreams that He gives, and brings us safely to wakefulness each morning with the promise of His company. The same troubled king David who struggled through the night watches determined, "O Lord, in the morning you hear my voice; in the morning I plead my case to you, and watch" (Psalm 5:3). We watch for Him, yes. And He comes.

Gott spricht zu jedem nur, eh er ihn macht

God speaks to every person before He makes him,
then silently walks with him out of the night.

Those words before anyone comes into being,
those cloudy words are:
Follow your senses.
Go to the limits of your longing.
Embody me.

Behind everything shall rise a flame
so that its shadow is great enough to hide me.

Let everything happen to you: beauty and terror.
Just keep moving. No emotion should be too far-fetched.
Do not separate from me.

Nearby is the land they call life.
You will know it by its sincerity.

Give me your hand.

RAINER MARIA RILKE, *The Book of Hours,* I, 59

LAUDS LITURGY

THE INVOCATION

    All: O Lord God of hosts, hear my prayer; give ear, O God of Jacob!

    Behold our shield, O God; look on the face of Your anointed.

    For a day in Your courts is better than a thousand elsewhere.

    I would rather be a doorkeeper in the house of my God than live in the tents of wickedness.

    For the Lord God is a sun and shield; He bestows favor and honor.

    No good thing does the Lord withhold from those who walk uprightly.

(Psalm 84:8–11)

THE GREETING

    One: Grace to you and peace from God our Father and the Lord Jesus Christ, who gave Himself for our sins to set us free from the present evil age, according to the will of our God and Father, to whom be the glory forever and ever.

    All: Amen.

(Galatians 1:3–5)

THE LAUDS REFRAIN

I am in all things na - ked. Spi - rit clothe me in the light.

PSALM 130 *(sung in unison)*

Out of the depths I cry to you O / Lord. * Lord \ hear my / voice.

Let Your ears be at/tentive
   *to the voice of my \suppli/cations!

If You, O Lord, should mark in/iquities,
   *Lord, who \could /stand?

But there is forgiveness with /You,
   *so that You may \be re/vered.

I wait for the /Lord,
   *my soul waits, and in His \word I /hope.

My soul waits for the Lord more than those who watch for the /morning,
   *more than those who watch \for the /morning.

O Israel, hope in the Lord! For with the Lord there is steadfast /love,
  *and with Him is great power \to re/deem.

GLORIA IN EXCELSIS *(sung in like manner)*

Glory to God in the /highest,
  *and on earth peace to people \of good /will.

We praise You. We /bless You.
  *We adore You. We glorif\y /You.

We give thanks to You for Your great /glory.
  *Alle\lu/ia.

Glory to God in the /highest,
  *and on earth peace to people \of good /will.

THE LAUDS REFRAIN *(see above)*

READING ZECHARIAH'S SONG

One: Now the time came for Elizabeth to give birth, and she bore a son. Her neighbors and relatives heard that the Lord had shown His great mercy to her, and they rejoiced with her.

On the eighth day they came to circumcise the child, and they were going to name him Zechariah after his father. But his mother said, "No; he is to be called John." They said to her, "None of your relatives has this name." Then they began motioning to his father to find out what name he wanted to give him. He asked for a writing tablet and wrote, "His name is John." And all of them were amazed. Immediately his mouth was opened and his tongue freed, and he began to speak, praising God. Fear came over all their neighbors, and all these things were talked about throughout the entire hill country of Judea. All who heard them pondered them and said, "What then will this child become?" For, indeed, the hand of the Lord was with him.

Then his father Zechariah was filled with the Holy Spirit and spoke this prophecy:

All: "Blessed be the Lord God of Israel, for He has looked favorably on His people and redeemed them. He has raised up a mighty savior for us in the house of His servant David, as He spoke through the mouth of His holy prophets from of old, that we would be saved from our enemies and from the hand of all who hate us.

Thus He has shown the mercy promised to our ancestors, and has remembered His holy covenant, the oath that He swore to our ancestor Abraham, to grant us that we, being rescued from the hands of our enemies, might serve Him without fear, in holiness and righteousness before Him all our days.

And you, child, will be called the prophet of the Most High; for you will go before the Lord to prepare His ways, to give knowledge of salvation to His people by the forgiveness of their sins. By the tender mercy of our God, the dawn from on high will break upon us, to give light to those who sit in darkness and in the shadow of death, to guide our feet into the way of peace."

(Luke 1: 57–79)

THE LAUDS REFRAIN *(see above)*

SILENCE Ω

HYMN: IN THE MORNING WHEN I RISE

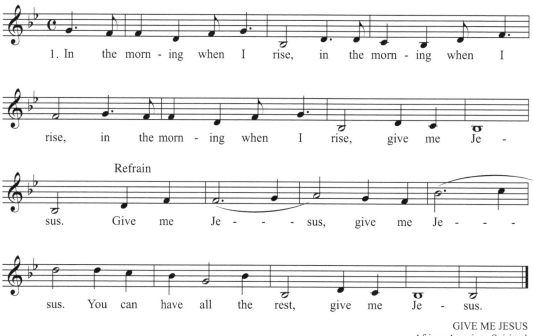

1. In the morn - ing when I rise, in the morn - ing when I rise, in the morn - ing when I rise, give me Je - sus.

Refrain

Give me Je - - - sus, give me Je - - - sus. You can have all the rest, give me Je - sus.

GIVE ME JESUS
African American Spiritual

2. Dark midnight was my cry, dark midnight was my cry, dark midnight was my cry, give me Jesus. Refrain

3. Just about the break of day, . . . Give me Jesus. Refrain

4. Oh, and when I come to die, . . . Give me Jesus. Refrain

5. And when I want to sing, . . . Give me Jesus. Refrain

THE LORD'S PRAYER Ω

THE PRAYERS Ω

THE LAUDS REFRAIN *(see above)*

THE SENDING
> **One:** God be in your head and in your understanding.
> God be in your eyes and in your looking.
> God be in your mouth and in your speaking.
> God be in your heart and in your thinking.
> God be at your end and at your departing.
> **All:** Amen.

In the strictest tradition, monastic communities gather for prayer eight times a day, every day. Within a week, they pray through the entire Psalter. The list below provides Psalm suggestions for Lauds, for use by communities desiring to use these liturgies in praying the Divine Office upon successive days:

Psalms 5, 28, 35, 42, 46, 50, 62, 63, 64, 66, 84, 89, 91, 92, 95, 96, 97, 98, 99, 100, 116, 134, 145, 146, 147, 148, 149, 150

PRIME

The day is lit. Choose your course.

My heart pounds
in Your rhythm,
syncopate my life, O God.

PRIME REFRAIN

Prime is the first hour of the day between the dawn of Lauds and the mid-morning hour of Terce. The day has fully emerged from the night, and the movement of the sun is discernable. This light has intention, taking, as it rises, a long slow look at a fresh Eden.

For many, this is the hour when one is finally fully awake and charged, even if one has been stumbling around out of bed for some time. To stop and pray at this time is to set the course of a day that will go awry otherwise, possibly setting in motion a chain of days without purpose.

Henry David Thoreau warned, "Most men lead lives of quiet desperation and go to the grave with the song still in them."[17] Such desperate lives do not come in a package, but are built day by day—a long progression toward meaning or toward emptiness. Greek myths tell of Prime hours marked by lives of interminable, pointless repetition. Cursed to roll a huge boulder up a hill only to watch it roll back down, Sisyphus repeats his drudgery throughout eternity. The lot of Prometheus is more tyrannical, because it threatens endlessly refreshed suffering: while Prometheus is bound to a rock, he is eviscerated each day by a great eagle, only to heal through the night. The death and resurrection of Christ turns this mockery upside down: each day is a new possibility for restoration to the image of God in which we were created.

The soundtrack of Prime is the drumming of

our hearts. The hour knows no bounds. It is long enough from night to deny its threat, and to allow belief in our own immortality. So, with bravado more than courage, we attempt things that appear overambitious as the day wears on. Yet great vision can be discerned, and great things set in motion at this hour. If dawn is the epiphany of a nascent idea, then Prime is that thought in its fruition, with all the fervor that accompanies big plans. The threat of this hour is not so much that one will be reckless, but rather that one will spend the energy unique to this hour on inadequate or dissipated goals. The emphasis of "choose your course" is not just on choosing the best path ahead, but on the importance of stopping to choose in the first place.

How does one, at arguably the least informed stage of one's adulthood, make such crucial choices? The first verse of Psalm 139 gives a strategic answer: "O Lord, you have searched me and known me." One is promised the Holy Spirit not so much as Comforter here, but as constant, omniscient Advisor. Along with the power to *do* comes the infectious confidence in our own grandeur and resistance to intrusion. Still, the goal is not a controlled life that we might conceive, but an abundant life only God can imagine. The result of ignoring God's higher thoughts for our lives produces the converse of enthusiasm—a hypocritical and free-floating anger at God that our lives are not turning out as we planned.

The gift of this hour is its infinite repetition, and its value is determined by whether we seize the day or are bored by its endless familiarity. Prayers during Prime, no matter how brief—perhaps prayed during the commute toward work—ought to be for God's direction, to listen for the whisper that Isaiah promises in 30:21 "And when you turn to the right or when you turn to the left, your ears shall hear a word behind you, saying, 'This is the way; walk in it.'"

It was the conviction of the early Benedictines

that just to stop for a moment was enough to re-
order the course of one's day, and to make each
movement of the day one step in a long unbroken
line of prayer. One begins to understand the possibility of prayer without ceasing, when it is not
the actions that one changes but rather the intention behind those actions. Artist Ed Knippers was
asked by his students if it is possible to love work
too much. "No," he replied, "but it is possible to
love God too little."[18]

Da neigt sich die Stunde und ruhrt mich an

The hour strikes; its clear, metallic gong
rings inside of me. My senses resonate.
I realize, I can,
and I take hold of and sculpt the coming day.

Nothing in my life has ever been finished
without me first imagining it.
All becoming stands still without me.

My visions are ripe, and like a bride one has chosen
every man receives what he's desired.
No idea is too small for me, I love it no matter what.
I paint it on a background of gold,
make it large and hold it high,
even though I don't know yet, whose soul it will excite.

RAINER MARIA RILKE, *The Book of Hours*, I, I

PRIME LITURGY

THE INVOCATION

All: O God, the sun has risen. With it, lift up our hearts and prepare us for all that the day will bring. Be with us in our deliberate and humble beginning of the day, in work as in prayer. Amen.

THE GREETING

All: May the grace of the Lord Jesus Christ, the love of God, and the communion of the Holy Spirit be with us all.

(2 Corinthians 13:13)

THE PRIME REFRAIN

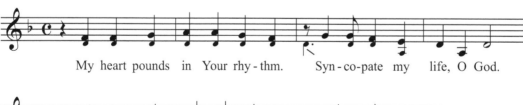

My heart pounds in Your rhy-thm. Syn-co-pate my life, O God.

My heart pounds in Your rhy-thm. Syn-co-pate my life.

PSALM 95:1–7A *(sung antiphonally on a single tone)*

† O come, let us sing to the Lord; let us make a joyful noise to the rock of our salvation!
  ‡ Let us come into His presence with thanksgiving; let us make a joyful noise to Him
    with songs of praise!

† For the Lord is a great God, and a great King above all gods.
  ‡ In His hand are the depths of the earth; the heights of the mountains are His also.

† The sea is His, for He made it, and the dry land, which His hands have formed.
  ‡ Come, let us worship and bow down, let us kneel before the Lord, our Maker!

† For He is our God,
  ‡ and we are the people of His pasture, and the sheep of His hand.

GLORIA PATRI *(sung in like manner)*

† Glory to the Father and to the Son and to the Holy Spirit.
  ‡ As it was in the beginning, is now and ever shall be. Amen.

THE PRIME REFRAIN *(see above)*

Those who had arrested Jesus took him to Caiaphas the high priest, in whose house the scribes and the elders had gathered. But Peter was following him at a distance, as far as the courtyard of the high priest; and going inside, he sat with the guards in order to see how this would end. Now the chief priests and the whole council were looking for false testimony against Jesus so that they might put him to death, but they found none, though many false witnesses came forward. At last two came forward and said, "This fellow said, 'I am able to destroy the temple of God and to build it in three days.'" The high priest stood up and said, "Have you no answer? What is it that they testify against you?" But Jesus was silent. Then the high priest said to Him, "I put you under oath before the living God, tell us if you are the Messiah, the Son of God." Jesus said to him, "You have said so. But I tell you, from now on you will see the Son of Man seated at the right hand of Power and coming on the clouds of heaven."

(Matthew 26:57–64)

To all Christians—religious, clerics and laymen, men and women, to all who dwell in the entire world, Friar Frances, their servant and subject, offers submission with reverence, true peace from Heaven, and sincere charity in the Lord.

Since I am the servant of all, I am bound to serve all and administer the sweet-smelling words of my Lord. Whence considering in mind, that since personally on account of the infirmity and debility of my body, I cannot visit each of you, I have proposed by these present letters and announcements to repeat to you the words of Our Lord Jesus Christ.

Let us therefore love God and adore Him with a pure heart and a pure mind, since He Himself, seeking such above all, has said: "True adorers will adore the Father in spirit and in truth." For "it is proper" that all, "who adore Him, adore" Him "in the spirit of truth." And let us offer

Him praises and prayers "day and night" by saying, "Our Father who art in Heaven," since "it is proper that" we "always pray and not fail to do what we might."

(St. Francis of Assisi, A Letter to the Faithful, c. 1216–1226 CE)

THE PRIME REFRAIN *(see above)*

SILENCE Ω

HYMN: AWAKE, MY SOUL, AND WITH THE SUN

A - wake, my soul, and with the sun thy dail - y stage of

du - ty run. Shake off dull sloth, and joy - ful

rise to pay the morn - ing sac - ri - fice.

OLD HUNDRETH
Louis Bourgeois, 1510-1561

2. All praise to Thee, who safe hast kept and hast refreshed me while I slept.
   Grant, Lord, when I from death shall wake, I may of endless light partake.

3. Lord, I my vows to Thee renew. Disperse my sins as morning dew;
   Guard my first springs of thought and will; and with thyself my spirit fill.

4. Direct, control, suggest, this day, all I design or do or say,
   That all my powers, with all their might, in Thy sole glory may unite.

5. Praise God, from whom all blessings flow. Praise Him, all creatures here below.
   Praise Him above, ye heavenly host. Praise Father, Son, and Holy Ghost.

(Thomas Ken, 1637–1711)

THE LORD'S PRAYER Ω

THE PRAYERS Ω

THE PRIME REFRAIN *(see above)*

THE SENDING

One: Into this new day, with all it holds and all it brings, go forth in peace.
All: May Christ be with us. Amen.

In the strictest tradition, monastic communities gather for prayer eight times a day, every day. Within a week, they pray through the entire Psalter. The list below provides Psalm suggestions for Prime, for use by communities desiring to use these liturgies in praying the Divine Office upon successive days:

Psalms 1, 2, 6, 7, 8, 9, 10, 11, 12, 13, 14, 15, 16, 17, 18, 19, 20, 21, 22, 23, 24, 25, 26, 51, 52, 54, 71, 72, 93, 107, 108, 117, 118, 119, 144

TERCE

The light climbs. The worker pauses.

I worship You
with primal joy,
Holy Spirit,
Living God.

TERCE REFRAIN

T he light of Terce is bright, a sharp spotlight on our work. We have found the rhythm of a focus that has snapped into place, and the last intuition we have is to stop. And yet.

Benedict urged stopping at this hour precisely to say, *this work is not my purpose. My purpose is to praise God*. In fact, monks are encouraged to drop their work tools wherever they are, whatever they are doing, when the bell for Prime rings, to remember God's presence, and to acknowledge, as Rabbi Abraham Heschel put it, "Just to be is a blessing. Just to live, is holy."

This hour corresponds to the season beginning with Pentecost. Imagine how the disciples, knowing that Jesus had resurrected from the dead and given them a great commission, were charged with the seriousness and fervor of the task ahead. And yet they were required to wait. And wait. And wait. The Spirit finally descended on them at the third hour: the hour of Terce (Acts 2:15) the same hour, only a few months before, in which Jesus was crucified (Mark 15:25).

"The man who can articulate the movements of his inner life . . . is able slowly and consistently to remove the obstacles that prevent the Spirit from entering," counsels Henri Nouwen in his book *The Wounded Healer*. "He is able to create space for Him whose heart is greater than his, whose eyes see more than his and whose hand can heal more than his."[19] If the fire for work comes from our own bellies, we set in motion all things small: personal agendas, careers, professions that will prove inadequate at the end of our lives. As someone observed, no one ever regretted on his deathbed that he did not spend enough time at the office.

If the fire for our vocation comes from the Spirit, the result is miraculously fulfilling. We are taught that the secret to finding our lives is to lose them for the sake of the gospel (Matthew 10:39). Pentecost celebrates the miraculous arrival of the Holy Spirit, sent to give birth to the Church. The Spirit empowered Peter to share the story of the gospel with a crowd that had gathered because the ruckus of the Spirit's descent called loudly for their attention. At first, they charged the disciples with drunkenness, because their giddy joy was so uncontainable. When Peter explained what had happened, three thousand people "were added to their number." Three thousand, who became the Church. The spirit of Terce is one of solidarity, of empowering the community to work as one body for the kingdom—wherever we are in the world, alone or apart.

The Spirit that fell at Pentecost is the same spirit within which we live today. It is not something that we make room for in a corner of our hearts, like a piece of furniture. It is rather like stepping from a vacuum into open air. Terce marks a necessary stopping to call the Spirit down upon our work so that we may continue fueled not by calculation but by obedience, not by might but by the Spirit, not by duty but by joy. "He will yet fill your mouth with laughter," Job assures us, "and your lips with shouts of joy" (8:21).

The personality of Terce is characterized by this joy, joy that is prompted by gratitude. Joy is alive—a vivacious, sweet, tender, and powerful woman walking alongside to whom one can, every morning, express thanks for God's blessings.

Though the Hour's prayers are short, they are potent then, and they are merely a respite from the work that calls anew on the heels of those prayers. Artist Denise Klitsie says of the return to work: "the space in your head where you need to go in order to interact with the work is sacred. Allow yourself to say all the things in you to say. Go deep. Accept. Trust. Go into the images."[20] The *work* remaining to be done is the same as when we stopped to pray, but *we* are different when we return.

Ich glaube an Alles noch nie Gesagte

I am drawn to the things that have never been said.
I am determined to release these godly feelings
and not hold back
what others do not dare to ask.
If that's outrageous, my God, forgive.
All I am trying to say is this:

My very best offerings are spontaneous,
without hesitation or irritation,
in precisely the way children love You.

Like waters swell and ebb into the open sea,
I want to proclaim Your name, in mounting waves,
like no one has done before.
If that is audacious,
then let me be rude for the sake of my prayer,
which, sincere and solemn,
rises before Your veiled face.

RAINER MARIA RILKE, *The Book of Hours,* I, 12

TERCE LITURGY

THE INVOCATION

All: Come Holy Spirit, as You did at Pentecost. Come into our hearts. Come into our thoughts. Come into our work. Come into this day and purify us, preserve us, and give us the grace to produce the good works that will glorify Christ. Amen.

THE GREETING

One: To those who are called, who are beloved in God the Father and kept safe for Jesus Christ: May mercy, peace, and love be yours in abundance.

(Jude 1:1b–2)

THE TERCE REFRAIN

I wor-ship you with pri-mal joy, Ho-ly Spi-rit,

Li-ving God. I wor-ship you with pri-mal joy, Ho-ly Spi-rit.

PSALM 67 *(sung in unison)*

May God be gracious to us and bless us and make his face to shine u \ pon / us,

that Your way may be known upon earth, Your saving power among \all /nations.

Let the peoples praise You, O God; let all the \peoples /praise You.

Let the nations be glad and sing for joy, for You judge the peoples with equity
and guide the nations u\pon /earth.

Let the peoples praise You, O God; let all the \peoples /praise You.

The earth has yielded its increase; God, our God, \has /blessed us.

May God continue to bless us; let all the ends of the \earth /revere Him.

GLORIA PATRI *(sung in like manner)*

Glory be to the Father and the Son and the Holy Spirit. As it was in the beginning, is now
and ever shall be. \A/men.

THE TERCE REFRAIN *(see above)*

READINGS

Jesus taught us, saying: "Be on guard so that your hearts are not weighed down with dissipation and drunkenness and the worries of this life, and that day catch you unexpectedly, like a trap. For it will come upon all who live on the face of the whole earth. Be alert at all times, praying that you may have the strength to escape all these things that will take place, and to stand before the Son of Man."

(Luke 21:34–36)

As they were going along the road, someone said to Him, "I will follow you wherever you go."

And Jesus said to Him, "Foxes have holes, and birds of the air have nests; but the Son of Man has nowhere to lay His head." To another He said, "Follow me."

But he said, "Lord, first let me go and bury my father."

But Jesus said to him, "Let the dead bury their own dead; but as for you, go and proclaim the kingdom of God."

Another said, "I will follow you, Lord; but let me first say farewell to those at my home."

Jesus said to him, "No one who puts a hand to the plow and looks back is fit for the kingdom of God."

(Luke 9:57–62)

When the day of Pentecost had come, they were all together in one place. And suddenly from heaven there came a sound like the rush of a violent wind, and it filled the entire house where they were sitting. Divided tongues, as of fire, appeared among them, and a tongue rested on each of them. All of them were filled with the Holy Spirit and began to speak in other languages, as the Spirit gave them ability.

Now there were devout Jews from every nation under heaven living in Jerusalem. And at this sound the crowd gathered and was bewildered, because each one heard them speaking in the native language of each. Amazed and astonished, they asked, "Are not all these who are speaking Galileans? And how is it that we hear, each of us, in our own native language? Parthians, Medes, Elamites, and residents of Mesopotamia, Judea and Cappadocia, Pontus and Asia, Phrygia and Pamphylia, Egypt and the parts of Libya belonging to Cyrene, and visitors from Rome, both Jews and proselytes, Cretans and Arabs—in our own languages we hear them speaking about God's deeds of power." All were amazed and perplexed, saying to one another, "What does this mean?"

(Acts 2:1–12)

THE TERCE REFRAIN *(see above)*

SILENCE Ω

HYMN: THIS IS MY FATHER'S WORLD

TERRA PATRIS
Franklin L. Sheppard, 1852-1930

2. This is my Father's world; the birds their carols raise;
   The morning light, the lily white, declare their maker's praise.
   This is my Father's world; He shines in all that's fair.
   In the rustling grass, I hear Him pass; He speaks to me everywhere.

3. This is my Father's world; Oh, let me not forget
   That though the wrong seems oft so strong, God is the ruler yet.
   This is my Father's world; why should my heart be sad?
   The Lord is king, let the heavens ring; God reigns, let earth be glad!

(Maltbie Babcock, 1858–1901)

THE LORD'S PRAYER Ω

THE PRAYERS Ω

THE TERCE REFRAIN *(see above)*

THE SENDING

One: Go in peace, called and sent as the Church of Christ in the world.
All: We go to serve Him in all we do.
One: May the grace of God and the love of Christ go with you.
All: Amen.

In the strictest tradition, monastic communities gather for prayer eight times a day, every day. Within a week, they pray through the entire Psalter. The list below provides Psalm suggestions for Terce, for use by communities desiring to use these liturgies in praying the Divine Office upon successive days:

Psalms 19, 20, 21, 22, 26, 27, 30, 31, 32, 33, 34, 39, 40, 41, 42, 43, 44, 45, 53, 54, 72, 79, 81, 82, 88, 94, 101, 118, 120, 121, 122

SEXT

The sun is overhead. The traveler reaches a crossroad.

My body's dust,

my soul eternal.

Give me courage for this hour.

SEXT REFRAIN

Noon is the hour when the sun is overhead, sizzling and merciless yet glorious with the fullness of God. At this, the sixth hour, Adam and Eve ate together of the forbidden tree: consuming the knowledge of good and evil in the same bite of the same fruit. Their disobedience would result in expulsion from the Garden and a break in fellowship with God; yet in response God set in motion a plan of unimagined intimacy—to walk among them as a man, to send His Spirit to live within them. Again, it was at the hour of Sext, when Christ hung on the cross to amend our sins, and a preternatural darkness fractured time. Day became night.

Sext is the dull center of ordinary time, the hazy clacking dry torpor of late summer, the mid-life crisis of our days. We are tempted to laziness and despair, to apathy and the heat-worn lethargy that accompanies it. At this hour, everything seems hard. Hard to keep the precarious hold on what remains of the day, hard to climb, hard to hold on, hard to let go, hard to be bothered. Potential and possibility hold more mockery than promise. In her seminal work on acedia, Kathleen Norris describes the threat of this state of mind, which is far more nefarious than mere indifference: "Not only does [acedia] make us unable to care, it takes away our ability to feel bad about that."[21]

Who can bear to look at the sun directly, who can look directly at this Hour? What do you do with a day—a life—that feels as though it has not even started until noon? All the morning hours of light and encouragement are gone, perhaps wasted, and remaining are the afternoon hours of paradox and challenge. Half of life is spent, and night is coming.

No wonder the Benedictines called Sext "the Hour of the noonday devil." Sext is also the Hour of intensity, however, when a surge of ambition and care wakes us from the poppy fields, when we are stirred by songwriter James Taylor's advice to "look up from your life."[22] Because of this tension, all drama peaks in this Hour, and David Steindl-Rast says, "At this turning point we decide the fate of our day and cumulatively of our lives."[23] At no other hour do we so poignantly feel our dual nature, made in the eternal image of God and yet confined to temporal life. There is the wisdom and intention, the desire for legacy, and yearning for purpose greater than ourselves that comes with age. And yet there is the soul-crushing practicality and disappointment that comes of the same experience. The edges have been knocked off of Prime's boundless enthusiasm and we are left at a crossroads where all choices are muddy.

However forlorn, impossible, or foolish our prospects are judged to be at this Hour, the prayers of Sext are to remind us that God prepares the way, and the door He has opened cannot be shut (Revelations 3:7). That way, in fact, is *made perfect* in the crucible of our thwarted plans. "Above all," counsels Teilhard de Chardin, "trust in the slow work of God. We are quite naturally impatient in everything to reach the end without delay. We should like to skip the intermediate stages. . . . Yet it is the law of all progress that it is made by passing through some stages of instability and that may take a very long time."[24] At the crest of this Hour, God works—crowbar and blowtorch—to unseal the heavy doors that we have built around our hearts with all our troubled strategies. When He breaks through, we must receive Him with all our might and abandon ourselves to His rescue.

Du, gestern Knabe, dem die Wirrnis kam

Yesterday you were a boy,
today blind passion makes your blood swell.

You do not mean to seek lust but joy;
you have been chosen as a groom
whose desire is only for his bride.

But the spirit of lust pulls at you,
even ordinary arms suggest nakedness.

Even pale cheeks on pious paintings
blush with strange appeal.
Desire twists like a snake,
rising to the beat of the tambourine.
Suddenly you are left alone
with hands that will betray you
unless your will delivers a miracle.

But news from God comes
rushing through dark alleys
into your heart.

RAINER MARIA RILKE, *The Book of Hours*, I, 38

SEXT LITURGY

THE INVOCATION

    All: O most merciful Redeemer, Friend, and Brother, may we know You more clearly, love You more dearly, and follow You more nearly, day by day. Amen.

THE GREETING

    One: May the peace of Christ be with you all.
    All: And also with you.

THE SEXT REFRAIN

My bo-dy's dust, my soul e-ter-nal. Give me cou-rage for this hour. My

bo-dy's dust, my soul e-ter-nal. Give me cou-rage for this hour.

PSALM 147 *(sung antiphonally on a single tone)*

† Praise the Lord! How good it is to sing praises to our God; for He is gracious,
and a song of praise is fitting.

    ‡ The Lord builds up Jerusalem; He gathers the outcasts of Israel.

† He heals the brokenhearted, and binds up their wounds.

    ‡ He determines the number of the stars; He gives to all of them their names.

† Great is our Lord, and abundant in power; His understanding is beyond measure.

    ‡ The Lord lifts up the downtrodden; He casts the wicked to the ground.

† Sing to the Lord with thanksgiving; make melody to our God on the lyre.

    ‡ He covers the heavens with clouds, prepares rain for the earth,

        makes grass grow on the hills.

† He gives to the animals their food, and to the young ravens when they cry.

    ‡ His delight is not in the strength of the horse,

        nor His pleasure in the speed of a runner;

† But the Lord takes pleasure in those who fear Him, in those who hope in His steadfast love.

    ‡ Praise the Lord, O Jerusalem! Praise your God, O Zion!

† For He strengthens the bars of your gates; He blesses your children within you.

    ‡ He grants peace within your borders; He fills you with the finest of wheat.

† He sends out his command to the earth; His word runs swiftly.

    ‡ He gives snow like wool; He scatters frost like ashes.

† He hurls down hail like crumbs—who can stand before His cold?

    ‡ He sends out His word, and melts them; He makes His wind blow,

        and the waters flow.

† He declares His word to Jacob, His statutes and ordinances to Israel.

    ‡ He has not dealt thus with any other nation; they do not know His ordinances.

        Praise the Lord!

GLORIA PATRI *(sung in like manner)*

> † Glory to the Father and to the Son and to the Holy Spirit.
>
> ‡ As it was in the beginning, is now and ever shall be. Amen.

THE SEXT REFRAIN *(see above)*

READINGS

Seek the Lord while He may be found, call upon Him while He is near; let the wicked forsake their way, and the unrighteous their thoughts; let them return to the Lord, that He may have mercy on them, and to our God, for He will abundantly pardon. For My thoughts are not your thoughts, nor are your ways My ways, says the Lord. For as the heavens are higher than the earth, so are My ways higher than your ways and My thoughts than your thoughts. For as the rain and the snow come down from heaven, and do not return there until they have watered the earth, making it bring forth and sprout, giving seed to the sower and bread to the eater, so shall My word be that goes out from My mouth; it shall not return to Me empty, but it shall accomplish that which I purpose, and succeed in the thing for which I sent it. For you shall go out in joy, and be led back in peace; the mountains and the hills before you shall burst into song, and all the trees of the field shall clap their hands.

(Isaiah 55:6–12)

When it was noon, darkness came over the whole land until three in the afternoon. At three o'clock Jesus cried out with a loud voice, "Eloi, Eloi, lama sabachthani?" which means, "My God, my God, why have you forsaken me?" When some of the bystanders heard it, they said, "Listen, he is calling for Elijah." And someone ran, filled a sponge with sour wine, put it on a stick, and gave it to Him to drink, saying, "Wait, let us see whether Elijah will come to take Him down."

(Mark 15:33–36)

THE SEXT REFRAIN *(see above)*

SILENCE Ω

HYMN: PRAISE TO THE LORD, THE ALMIGHTY, THE KING OF CREATION

1. Praise to the Lord, the al-might-y the King of cre-a - tion. O my soul

praise him for he is your health and sal - va - tion. Let all who hear

now to his tem - ple draw near, join-ing in glad a - dor - a - tion.

LOBE DEN HERRN
Traditional German melody

2. Praise to the Lord, who o'er all things is wondrously reigning
   And as on wings of an eagle, uplifting, sustaining.
   Have you not seen all that is needful has been
   Sent by His gracious ordaining?

3. Praise to the Lord, who will prosper your work and defend you;
   Surely His goodness and mercy shall daily attend you.
   Ponder anew what the Almighty can do,
   If with His love He befriend you.

4. Praise to the Lord! Oh, let all that is in me adore Him.
   All that has life and breath, come now with praises before Him.
   Let the amen sound from his people again.
   Gladly forever adore Him.

   (Joachim Neander, 1650–1680/trans. Catherine Winkworth, 1829–1878)

THE LORD'S PRAYER Ω

THE PRAYERS Ω

THE SEXT REFRAIN *(see above)*

THE SENDING

> **One:** Go forth, remember who you are and to whom you belong.
>
> **All:** Amen.

In the strictest tradition, monastic communities gather for prayer eight times a day, every day. Within a week, they pray through the entire Psalter. The list below provides Psalm suggestions for Sext, for use by communities desiring to use these liturgies in praying the Divine Office upon successive days:

Psalms 30, 40, 41, 52, 53, 54, 55, 56, 57, 60, 61, 62, 63, 64, 65, 66, 67, 68, 69, 70, 71, 72, 73, 83, 84, 85, 86, 87, 88, 89, 103, 118

NONE

Shadows grow. No one lives forever.

When daylight wanes
and shadows lengthen,
to forgive is to make whole.

NONE REFRAIN

How beautiful this dappled, soft hour of light, and yet heartbreaking. Grey at the temples, the hour of None is melancholy, a time to ponder things we thought would always be with us. The loss of our plans, our parents, our pains have eroded confidence in the ability to conquer time. There is not much light left to the day to work or read or see by, nor to the seasons of our lives. Mortality is undeniable, and even those who are most ambitious—or deepest in denial—must admit time is short before winter. A lonely hour, None is when monks pray alone in their cells for a holy death.

We crave contact with something transcendent at this time of day precisely because temporal things are dissolving into shadow. None is the second most populated hour at coffee houses, whether for stimulant or company, it hardly matters. Though natural to reflect on loss, Teilhard de Chardin urges hopeful patience: "Only God could say what this new spirit gradually forming within you will be. Give our Lord the benefit of believing that His hand is leading you, and accept the anxiety of feeling yourself in suspense and incomplete."[25] Suspense is natural to this, the ninth hour, when even Jesus Christ cried out to God "why hast thou forsaken me?" Receiving no answer, He sighed, "it is finished," and breathed His last. Perhaps the torpor common to this time of day is a soul-memory of that black hour marking the death of our Savior.

The None hour is an hour of sleepy prayer, when the light plays among the shadows it creates and we are haunted by old dreams. Poet Henry David Thoreau's oft-quoted sentiments become our standard of judgment: "I wanted to live deep and suck out all the marrow of life, To put to rout all that was not life and not, when I had come to die, discover that I had not lived."[26] This is the hour that tests determinations such as these, and the gentle challenge of None is not to give up, for there is time left. Now, at the hour when things that we have relied upon fail, first look to what endures: "Jesus Christ is the same yesterday and today and forever" (Hebrews 13:8).

Trust is an important attribute of this hour. "Wait for the Lord; be strong, and let your heart take courage; wait for the Lord!" the Psalmist urges (27:14). For some, None brings temptations to anxiety, of turning inward to critique and mourn lost youth, or worse, to try to recapture it. But this is a season to turn one's mind toward legacies with eternal value: "The first and most basic task of the Christian leader in the future," says Henri Nouwen in *The Wounded Healer*, "will be to lead his people out of the land of confusion and into the land of hope. Therefore, he must first have the courage to be an explorer of the new territory in himself, and to articulate his discoveries as a service to the inward generation."[27] So, the past may be transformed from failure into gift.

South African leader Nelson Mandela, when asked upon his release from prison if he feared death, quoted William Shakespeare: "Cowards die many times before their deaths; the valiant never taste of death but once. Of all the wonders that I yet have heard, it seems to me most strange that men should fear; seeing that death—a necessary end—will come when it will come." Embrace this, said Mandela, and you will "disappear under a cloud of glory."[28]

At this hour, we are urged to shift our thinking from what we have left unachieved to what we might yet leave behind, and to apply our energies to forgiveness and generosity. When the disciples criticized a woman who had lived a sinful life for pouring an expensive bottle of perfume on Jesus' feet, He rebuked them with what is surely a strategy for facing eternity without fear: "For this reason I say to you her sins, which are many, have been forgiven, for she loved much" (Luke 7:47 NAS). So then, in the day toward which we all journey, it may not be asked of us whether we sinned, but whether we loved.

Ich liebe meines Wesens Dunkelstunden

I love those dark hours, those melancholy ones,
when all my senses are alert.
I have found in those hours,
like reading someone else's letters,
my ordinary life has been lived a hundred times.
It is a legend that reaches beyond me.
I realize the promise of a second
eternal life.

I am like a tree
that grows next to a grave
holding high in its mighty branches the dream
a lost boy once dreamt though he lies in my roots' embrace
forever gone in sadness and lament.

RAINER MARIA RILKE, *The Book of Hours*, I, 5

NONE LITURGY

THE INVOCATION

    All: Come, Holy Spirit. Be with us in the waning of the day. As shadows lengthen, strengthen our resolve to be Christ to all we meet. Amen.

THE GREETING

    One: Peace be with you. May the presence of the Risen Christ strengthen and sustain you.

    All: And so may it be with you.

THE NONE REFRAIN

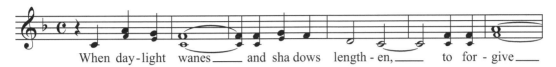

When day-light wanes___ and sha dows length - en,___ to for - give___

___ is to make whole.___ When day - light wanes___ and sha-dows

length - en,___ to for - give___ is to be whole.

PSALM 121 *(sung in unison)*

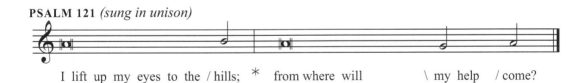

I lift up my eyes to the / hills; * from where will \ my help / come?

My help comes from the /Lord,
*who made heaven \and /earth.

He will not let your foot be /moved;
>   *He who keeps you \will not /slumber.

He who keeps /Israel
>   *will neither slumber \nor /sleep.

The Lord is your /keeper;
>   *the Lord is your shade at \your right /hand.

The sun shall not strike you by /day,
>   *nor the moon \by /night.

The Lord will keep you from all /evil;
>   *He will keep \your /life.

The Lord will keep your going out and your coming /in
>   *from this time forth and for\ever/more.

GLORIA IN EXCELSIS *(sung in like manner)*

Glory to God in the /highest,
>   *and on earth peace to people \of good /will.

We praise you. We /bless you.
>   *We adore you. We glori\fy /you.

We give thanks to you for your great /glory.
>   *Alle\lu/ia.

Glory to God in the /highest,
>   *and on earth peace to people \of good /will.

THE NONE REFRAIN *(see above)*

READINGS

Then Jesus told His disciples, "If any want to become My followers, let them deny themselves and take up their cross and follow Me. For those who want to save their life will lose it, and those who lose their life for My sake will find it. For what will it profit them if they gain the whole world but forfeit their life? Or what will they give in return for their life?"

(Matthew 16:24–26)

For the kingdom of heaven is like a landowner who went out early in the morning to hire laborers for his vineyard. After agreeing with the laborers for the usual daily wage, he sent them into his vineyard. When he went out about nine o'clock, he saw others standing idle in the marketplace; and he said to them, "You also go into the vineyard, and I will pay you whatever is right." So they went. When he went out again about noon and about three o'clock, he did the same. And about five o'clock he went out and found others standing around; and he said to them "Why are you standing here idle all day?"

They said to him, "Because no one has hired us." He said to them, "You also go into the vineyard." When evening came, the owner of the vineyard said to his manager, "Call the laborers and give them their pay, beginning with the last and then going to the first."

When those hired about five o'clock came, each of them received the usual daily wage.

Now when the first came, they thought they would receive more; but each of them also received the usual daily wage. And when they received it, they grumbled against the landowner, saying, "These last worked only one hour, and you have made them equal to us who have borne the burden of the day and the scorching heat."

But he replied to one of them, "Friend, I am doing you no wrong; did you not agree with me for the usual daily wage? Take what belongs to you and go; I choose to give to this last the same as I give to you. Am I not allowed to do what I choose with what belongs to me? Or are you envious because I am generous?" So the last will be first, and the first will be last.

(Matthew 20:1–16)

After this, when Jesus knew that all was now finished, He said (in order to fulfill the Scripture), "I am thirsty." A jar full of sour wine was standing there. So they put a sponge full of the wine on a branch of hyssop and held it to His mouth. When Jesus had received the wine, He said, "It is finished." Then He bowed His head and gave up His spirit.

(John 19:28–30)

THE NONE REFRAIN *(see above)*

SILENCE Ω

HYMN: BE THOU MY VISION

1. Be thou my vision, O Lord of my heart; naught be all else to me, save that thou art: thou my best thought both by day and by night, wak-ing or sleep-ing, thy pre-sence my light.

SLANE
Traditional Irish melody

2. Be Thou my wisdom, and Thou my true word;
   I ever with Thee and Thou with me, Lord.
   Thou my soul's shelter, and Thou my high tower,
   Raise Thou me heavenward, O Power of my power.

3. Riches I heed not, nor vain, empty praise,
   Thou mine inheritance, now and always;
   Thou and Thou only, the first in my heart,
   Great God of heaven, my treasure Thou art.

4. Light of my soul, after victory won,
   May I reach heaven's joys, O heaven's Son.
   Heart of my own heart, whatever befall,
   Still be my vision, O Ruler of all.

(Ancient Irish; trans. Mary E. Byrne, 1905; versed by Eleanor H. Hull, 1912)

THE LORD'S PRAYER Ω

THE PRAYERS Ω

THE NONE REFRAIN *(see above)*

THE SENDING

One: The Lord bless us and keep us. The Lord make His face shine upon us and be gracious to us. The Lord look upon us with favor and give us peace.
Go in peace, serve the Lord.
All: Thanks be to God.

In the strictest tradition, monastic communities gather for prayer eight times a day, every day. Within a week, they pray through the entire Psalter. The list below provides Psalm suggestions for None, for use by communities desiring to use these liturgies in praying the Divine Office upon successive days:

Psalms 31, 32, 43, 58, 59, 74, 75, 88, 95, 96, 97, 98, 99, 100, 101, 102, 103, 104, 105, 106, 107, 108, 109, 110, 111, 108, 118

MUSICAL ARRANGEMENTS

The Vespers Refrain

The sun re-cedes, we wor-ship You. We eat, we pray, we drink, we sing. Hi
nei mah tove __ u - mah na' - im she - vet a - chim gam ya - chad.

C Instrument

Variation 1

The Vespers Refrain

Variation 2

Variation 3

The Compline Refrain

The Compline Refrain

The Vigils Refrain

Here   I   am,   here   I   am,   Your   ser - vant   I   am.

Here   I   am,   here   I   am,   Your   ser - vant,   I   AM.

C Instrument

Variation 1

Copyright © 2010 by Clayton J. Schmit and Lauralee Farrer

The Vigils Refrain

Variation 2

Variation 3

The Lauds Refrain

I am in all things na - ked. Spir - it clothe me in the light. I
am in all things na - ked. Spir - it clothe me in the light.

C Instrument

Variation 1

The Lauds Refrain

The Prime Refrain

The Prime Refrain

The Prime Refrain

The Terce Refrain

The Terce Refrain

Variation 2

Variation 3

The Sext Refrain

The Sext Refrain

Variation 1

Variation 2

The Sext Refrain

Variation 3

The None Refrain

The None Refrain

The None Refrain

Variation 3

ENDNOTES

Preface: Eternity in Our Hearts

1   Thomas Merton, *The Seven Storey Mountain* (Harcourt Brace Jovanovich, 1998), 362.

2   Thomas Merton, *Wisdom of the Desert* (New Directions, 1970), 3-24.

3   Craig Barnes, *Sacred Thirst: Meeting God in the Desert of Our Longings* (Zondervan Publishing House, 2001), 20.

4   Ray S. Anderson, *Exploration into God: Sermonic Meditations on the Book of Ecclesiastes* (Wipf & Stock Publishers, 2006).

5   Lucien Hervé, *Architecture of Truth* (Phaidon Press, 2001).

How To Use This Book

6   Statement provided by Fuller Theological Seminary student Olga Lah.

7   Graham Hughes, *Worship as Meaning* (Cambridge University Press, 2003), 151.

8   Tom F. Driver, *The Magic of Ritual* (HarperCollins, 1991), 7.

A Holy Space

9   White, James F., *Introduction to Christian Worship* (Abingdon Press, 2000), 81.

Time Is Not Money

10 Iron & Wine, *Our Endless Numbered Days* (Sub Pop, 2004).

11 James B. Ashbrook, *Paul Tillich in Conversation: Psychotherapy, Religion, Culture, History* (Graduate Theological Foundation of Indiana, 1988), 112-14.

12 Phyllis Tickle, "What Drew Me In and Kept Me Practicing Fixed-Hour Prayer," *Explore Faith*, http://www.explorefaith.org/prayer/fixed/tickle.html (accessed 11/2/09).

13 Eugene Peterson, *The Jesus Way* (Eerdmans, 2007), 163.

The Hours

14 David Scholer, "It Is about God, Not about Us," Baccalaureate Service, Fuller Theological Seminary, June 4, 2008.

15 Vaclav Havel, "It Is I Who Must Begin," in *Teaching with Fire: Poetry That Sustains the Courage to Teach*, ed. Sam M. Intrator and Megan Scribner (Jossey Bass, 2003), 188.

16 Thomas Ken, "Awake, My Soul, and With the Sun," public domain, 1674.

17 Henry David Thoreau, *Walden* (E.P. Dutton & Co, 1904), 30.

18 Overheard, Edward Knippers, for more, see www.edknippers.com.

19 Henri Nouwen, *The Wounded Healer: Ministry in Contemporary Society* (Image Books, 1979), 38.

20 Overheard, Denise Louise Klitsie, for more, see http://web.mac.com/meldklitsie/iWeb/Paintings/Studio.html.

21 Kathleen Norris, *Acedia & Me: A Marriage, Monks, and a Writer's Life* (Riverhead, 2008), 45.

22 James Taylor, "Up from Your Life," *Hourglass* (Sony 1997), 9.

23 David Steindl-Rast, O.S.B., and Sharon Lebell, *Music of Silence: A Sacred Journey through the Hours of the Day* (Ulysses Press, 2002), 70.

24 Teilhard de Chardin, "Patient Trust," from Michael G. Harter S.J., *Hearts on Fire: Praying with Jesuits* (Loyola Press, 2005), 102.

25 Ibid.

26 Thoreau, *Walden*, 87.

27 Nouwen, *The Wounded Healer*, 41.

28 Nelson Mandela in "Oprah Interviews Nelson Mandela," *O, the Oprah Magazine*, April 2001 (Harpo, Inc., 2001), see http://www.oprah.com/article/omagazine/omag_200104_ocut (accessed 11/2/09).

GRATEFUL ACKNOWLEDGMENT

to William K. and Delores Brehm

to Fuller Theological Seminary, which houses
The Brehm Center for Worship, Theology, and the Arts

to those at the Brehm Center who helped make this happen—Fred and Dottie Davison,
Lynn Reynolds, Trent Pettit

to Susan Carlson Wood

to Rick Curtis, for embodying Benedict in ordinary life

to Carol, Kyrie, and Jacob Schmit, for their ceaseless prayers and endless songs

ABOUT THE CONTRIBUTORS

Clayton J. Schmit is the Arthur DeKruyter/Christ Church Oak Brook Professor of Preaching and the academic director of the Brehm Center for Worship, Theology, and the Arts at Fuller Theological Seminary. An accomplished choral music director and composer, his scholarly areas of expertise include homiletics, aesthetics of preaching and liturgy, and composing, conducting, and performing liturgical music.

Lauralee Farrer is an award-winning filmmaker and the president of Burning Heart Productions. She has been writing, producing, and directing professionally for over thirty years, and often lectures on issues of faith and art. She is the editor of *Theology, News & Notes* from Fuller Theological Seminary—a graduate institution for the study of theology, psychology, and intercultural studies.

Denise Louise Klitsie is a painter and illustrator who graduated from the Art Center College of Design in 1989. She spent seven years with Walt Disney Feature Animation as a layout artist, art-directed the independent feature *The Best Man in Grass Creek* (1999), and was a cinematographer on the documentary film *The Fair Trade*.

Martina Nagel is a cinematographer and screenwriter, with her master's degree from the Free University of Berlin in Germany. She worked for twelve years on documentaries by the BBC, designed and ran script clinics with Spark Productions in London, and is a published writer and lecturer.